When Home Is No Haven

WHEN HOME IS

Albert J. Solnit, M.D.

Barbara F. Nordhaus, M.S.W.

Ruth Lord, M.A.

Yale University Press

New Haven and London

Child

Placement

Issues

NO HAVEN

Copyright © 1992 by Yale University.
All rights reserved.
This book may not be reproduced, in
whole or in part, including illustrations, in any
form (beyond that copying permitted by Sections 107 and 108
of the U.S. Copyright Law and except by
reviewers for the public press), without written
permission from the publishers.

Designed by Sonia L. Scanlon.
Set in Janson type by Brevis Press.
Printed in the United States of America by
BookCrafters, Inc., Chelsea, Michigan.

Library of Congress Cataloging-in-Publication Data
Solnit, Albert J.
When home is no haven : child placement issues /
Albert J. Solnit, Barbara F. Nordhaus, Ruth Lord.
p.   cm.
Includes bibliographical references and index.
ISBN 0-300-05091-7 (cloth)
0-300-05931-0 (pbk.)
1. Foster home care—United States—Case
studies.   2. Adoption—United States—Case
studies.   3. Abused children—United States—
Family relationships—Case studies.   4. Foster
children—United States—Family relationships—
Case studies.   5. Child development—United
States—Case studies.   I. Nordhaus, Barbara F.
II. Lord, Ruth, 1922–   .   III. Title.
HV875.55.S66   1992
362.7'6—dc20   91-4904
CIP

The paper in this book meets the guidelines
for permanence and durability of the
Committee on Production Guidelines for Book
Longevity of the Council on Library Resources

10   9   8   7   6   5   4   3   2

We dedicate this book to the staff of
the Connecticut Department of Children
and Youth Services. We hope that these
case studies will offer useful knowledge to
those from whose experience and perseverance
we have learned so much.

As this book unfolded, we became aware that
we were writing it for other child experts as
well—nurses, pediatricians, child psychiatrists
and psychologists, and certain judges and
lawyers. We further include parents, students,
and scholars, who through their advocacy
are an essential resource for children.

Contents

Foreword

Decision making in child abuse and neglect cases is a difficult and complex process. Whether to remove a child from his or her home, whether to return to the home a child who has been abused, and whether to sever permanently a child's legal ties to his or her parents—all are awesome decisions. Collecting, assessing, and discussing all relevant data with an awareness of a child's sense of time is essential in formulating an optimal plan for the child.

The cases presented in this book are actual cases encountered on a daily basis in our work at the Connecticut State Department of Children and Youth Services. In many ways, these families and their situations represent ordinary situations that confront protective-service workers across the state. What is remarkable about them is the process that led to the permanent plans for these children. Although not remarkable, and often quite sad, the most realistic plan for a number of these children is not ideal but represents the best that is available at a given time. Furthermore, despite the best efforts of our collaborative group, we confront the limitations of our ability to make valid predictions.

Virtually every case discussed in this book involved group decision making that included administrators, supervisors, social workers, and consultants. Effective collaboration resulted in better planning for children and also in enhanced social work skills for our workers and hence greater job satisfaction. An essential ingredient for an effective collaborative process is mutual respect among all of the participants—managers, social workers, administrators, and consultants. In presenting their cases, social workers must feel confident that their work and their ideals will be given equal weight with those of the others in the group. This freedom to collaborate enables workers to receive maximum benefits from consultation and group meetings and ultimately results in better services for children.

Carole Porto, M.S.W.
Regional Administrator
Children's Protective Services

Preface

Our objective in writing this volume has been to provide a case-book that will be of practical value to those in the field of child placement. We emphasize the decision-making process involved in responding to the challenges of child neglect and abuse that require societal intervention. The process is rooted in the converging judgments that are the outcome of clinical evaluation, treatment planning, and case management.

Lamentably, our resources are always limited; the quality of treatment planning and case management depends on maximizing what is available in the best interests of the child. Often under conditions of stress, workers are faced with decisions that may profoundly change the lives of children and their parents. This can be a lonely, daunting responsibility. Collaboration with colleagues, supervisors, and consultants is essential. The book represents what we have learned from our coworkers, in the context of real cases that we have been privileged to study and evaluate with them.

In organizing the book, we have followed Bulletin #30, *Manual Volume 2* of Connecticut's Division of Protective Services *Standards for the Removal and Return of Children by the Department of Children and Youth Services*.* These standards, unofficially known as the Guidelines, became effective in 1981, having been developed in a collaborative effort between Connecticut's Department of Children and Youth Services† and the Child Study Center of Yale University. The Guidelines are in need of revision, and we hope that this casebook will represent a first step toward this end.

---

*See appendix 1.

†In the rest of the book we have used the term Child Protective Services (CPS) instead of Department of Children and Youth Services (DCYS), which is specific to Connecticut.

We offer the book as a possible source of additional support for front-line workers. We hope that it will be useful as a learning or reference tool for new workers and as a resource for those more experienced colleagues who seek to elaborate or refine their understanding. We are aware that problems of child placement continue to increase and to reflect the changing social conditions of our time. Escalating drug abuse, contagious diseases, and homelessness are some of the changes that make it all the more clear why we must update and revise our knowledge on a continuing basis.

Devoted and conscientious workers, given an overwhelming number of clients, cannot always invest as much time and effort in certain cases as they might wish to do. Furthermore, their job is often compounded by frustrations, such as the lack of suitable placement facilities and problems inherent in the judicial system. We describe various situations in detail in order to suggest constructive ways of looking at child placement problems. We have selected a wide range of cases that reflect the current reality. All names, dates, locations, and other identifying information have been changed. Although each case is inevitably unique, the process that goes into the attempt to resolve a problem is based on definable presumptions. We fully recognize that in too many instances "good" resolutions may not, in fact, exist. This makes it all the more important to realize that some alternatives are better than others.

Our central concern throughout is that the needs of children at different stages of development receive the highest priority. Our intent is to illustrate a useful merging of practice with principle and to increase the probability that there can be better times for children and their parents.

We are deeply grateful for the support, encouragement, and critical guidance of Ray Farrington, Joseph Goldstein, Charles Launi, Mark Marcus, Carole Porto, and Sally Provence. To these supporters and our collaborating colleagues in Protective Services, we acknowledge our thanks for the strengths of this book. We cannot burden them with any errors of omission or commission.

We wish also to thank our colleagues in the Bridgeport office, especially Sharon Martin, Lucy Foster, Tom Buch, Annie Christy, Barbara Frueler, Rita Gaspierik, Pat Goyette, Judy Grosner, Beverly Hubelbank, Mary Pollard, Phyllis Powell, Dolores Rice, and Andrea Routh. In addition, we thank Robert Budney, Dorothy Shaw, Amy Wheaton, Arthur Winokur, Dolores Woodward, and Rose Canneto.

We express our gratitude for their clinical expertise to our colleagues at the Child Study Center: Robert Evans, Martha Leonard, Eric Millman, Frank Ninivaggi, Ellis Perlswig, Carlos Salguero, John Schowalter, Fred Volkmar, Russell Wolfe, and Joseph Woolston. We further thank Frederica Brenneman, Steven Wizner, Thomas de Matteo, Donald Cohen, Sonja Goldstein, Kevin Grigsby, Jean Adnopoz, Catherine Cox, Steven Nagler, Dolores Gerzabek, and Dolores Gee.

And, finally, we acknowledge deep gratitude to Margrethe Cone for her painstaking and heartfelt attention to the many drafts of our manuscript. Her interest, help, and professional expertise were unparalleled.

1

Introduction:

A

Conceptual

Framework

The Historical Framework for Child Welfare Work

Violent physical abuse and murder of children by adults, often their parents, are as old as recorded history. Violence is aggression out of control. It represents a part of our biosocial heritage that has gone awry. Adults often react to the mistreatment of children by denying its existence or by overresponding with righteous indignation. The physical and sexual abuse of children by adults represents an activation of violence of which every human being is potentially capable. In Western society, at least for the past two hundred years, the expression of such violence has been condemned and prohibited by each community in its own way.*

The famous case of Mary Ellen in the United States in the late nineteenth century, in which an 8-year-old public ward was cruelly mistreated by the family to whom she was indentured, was not the first incident of child abuse to receive national attention (Coleman 1924; Gerbner et al. 1980). Although there were laws to protect children from parental abuse, this case, because of the publicity it received, "shocked many people into a greater awareness of this serious human problem, and it sparked the beginning of a massive crusade against child abuse" (Hiner 1979). Precipitated by the reactions to what happened to Mary Ellen and the realization that children did not have as much protection as domestic animals, the New York City Society for the Prevention of Cruelty to Children was organized in December 1874. Ironically, it was the American Society for the Prevention of Cruelty to Animals that succeeded in removing and protecting Mary Ellen from the abusing adults,

---

*To provide a brief conceptual overview of the child welfare field and its focus on issues of neglect and abuse, we have adapted excerpts from Solnit 1980.

after a charity worker, Mrs. Etta Angell Wheeler, was thwarted in the same attempt.

The abused or battered child was "rediscovered" in 1946 by a radiologist, Dr. John Caffey, when he reported an exotic new syndrome in which chronic subdural hematomas in infants often were associated with multiple atypical fractures of the long bones, namely the limbs and the ribs (Caffey 1946, 1957).

In 1962 the pediatrician C. Henry Kempe organized a multidisciplinary conference entitled "The Battered Child Syndrome." This "conference . . . set ablaze an impassioned outburst on behalf of abused children" (Radbill 1980, 17). The medical profession and the public could now acknowledge the previously denied existence of this age-old and continuing tragedy. Kempe's work supported the creation of laws that mandated how and by whom child abuse should be reported, as well as how the reporters were to be afforded legal immunity.

The Psychological Roots of Child Neglect and Abuse

Our society no longer tolerates physical abuse of children by adults, including their parents. Humanitarian considerations aside, such abuse represents a threat to the well-being of a community and to the values we place on children in our society. Although not all abusers have a history of being abused, parents may transmit to their children what they themselves have suffered. When such parents turn what they experienced passively into an active mode of behavior, doing to their children what was done to them in their own childhood, they and their children may become entrapped in the repetition of interactional patterns that distort and limit the children's normal development and capacities.

The point at which neglect becomes so severe as to endanger the child's life or well-being often is hard to ascertain, requiring the use of sound clinical judgment. If parents are depressed or suffer from the long-term effects of deprivation in their own childhood, they may lack the capacity to protect, nurture, guide, and stimulate their children. They may be unable to safeguard their children from physical harm or to form appropriate emotional attachments to them. In this way, certain deficits and deviations may be passed on from one generation to the next through the dynamics of family interaction.

Of course, the majority of such parents resolve their difficulties and attempt to ensure that their children will not suffer what they suffered.* They master the residue of their past deprivation or abuse by providing their children with what was not provided for them. They are able to offer sustained, affectionate care and guidance and to help their children confront the real world in socially constructive and satisfying ways. To a significant extent, the later outcome of childhood deprivation may reflect the freedom of some individuals to make choices that oppose their past experiences. In such instances, these individuals have found opportunities for sound health care, education, and employment that shape them as future parents. Similarly, continuity of cultural ties, social options, and pride in family or neighborhood may support individual mastery of the earlier deficits, deprivations, and disruptions of primary psychological relationships.

The Legal Framework for Child Welfare Work

Only in a prisonlike state could child abuse be abolished entirely. Because our democratic society assumes that parents will safeguard and nurture children, it has constitutionally guaranteed parental autonomy in providing care for them. It protects the integrity of family life associated with privacy, intimacy, and richness of emotional exchange and supports the diversity of differing life-styles. Such are our value preferences in a free society. These converge with children's developmental needs, as will be discussed in chapter 2.

---

*In their review of the literature, Kaufman and Zigler (1987) found that about 30 percent of individuals who had been abused as children subjected their offspring to similar mistreatment.

Since there is little or no agreement on what constitutes emotional and psychological neglect, the line between respecting and intruding into family privacy should be defined by physical abuse of the child, abandonment, or neglect that risks the physical safety of the child. Other forms of child neglect should be a challenge to the development of accessible voluntary services, not the basis for invading the privacy of the family.

Laws that require the reporting of child abuse and neglect and that protect those who report them from legal repercussions swept through this country in the 1950s and 1960s with unprecedented speed. They were designed mainly to safeguard the conscience of society as well as the legal vulnerability of those adults who were encouraged or mandated to report suspected cases of neglect or of abuse.

As Mnookin (1978) explains, "The need to discover and identify child victims of abuse is the compelling reason for devising a case finding tool such as the reporting law. . . . Failure to recognize the 'Battered Child Syndrome' could subject the child to additional or repeated injury or even death" (p. 315). Mnookin further notes that the purpose of mandatory reporting in child abuse cases is to ensure treatment of the child's present injuries and to protect the child from further abuse. Although all fifty states have enacted child abuse legislation, it varies in such matters as the standard for reporting, who is mandated to report, and how and to whom the report is made.

One negative aspect of the reporting laws is that family privacy frequently has been coercively invaded following reports stemming from life-style differences and from prejudice against minority, single-parent, or low-income families. The laws that were passed in each state to require mandatory reporting of neglect and abuse also guaranteed legal immunity to the reporters. This has greatly increased the number of complaints that must be investigated by the state. In most if not all states (Nagi 1975; Cohen and Sussman 1975) this epidemic of reporting has cast a wide net, bringing in, along with life-threatening cases of physical abuse, instances of suspected neglect and false reports. Reports that reflect implicit or explicit bias about life-style often can be harmful to the accused family.

In Connecticut, more than 1,000 new cases of child neglect and abuse are reported each month to the state registry from both mandated and non-mandated sources. Although more than 20 percent of these reports turn out to be false—a serious and threatening phenomenon in its own right—it is chilling to realize what a significant percentage of children in a state with a population of more than 3 million are subject to such inhumane conditions of life. In Connecticut in 1990 approximately 3,800 children were in out-of-home care at any given time. Of these, almost 50 percent, or 0.5 percent of the state's entire child population of 764,366, were in foster care. Of course it is difficult to estimate or document accurately the number of children actually caught up in this web.

Although the reporting laws protect the confidentiality of the reporter and provide immunity against suits for libel and slander, they rarely, if ever, provide more preventive, therapeutic, or protective resources for children and their families. In 1977 Congress passed the Child Abuse Prevention and Treatment Act, creating a national center for research on child abuse and neglect.

2

Developmental

Aspects

of

Children's

Needs

and

Rights

Child rearing can be viewed as the regulation by parents of the nurturance, stimulation, and frustration that their children experience. A closer consideration of the meaning of nurturance reveals its importance at every phase of development. The human child is born helpless and will perish if he or she is not nourished, protected, soothed, and stimulated by a person capable of providing such care on a continuing basis. What begins as biological helplessness leads to social and psychological attachment as a result of the interaction of the infant and the maternal person or persons. The infant progresses from biological dependency to an urgent need for affirmation, which is met and reinforced by predictable and dependable responses from his or her caretakers. Social development emerges as a result of the child's identifications with the primary "psychological parent." Goldstein, Freud, and Solnit (1973) acknowledge the difficulty of defining this term. They state that the child's attachment is based on day-to-day interaction and companionship and is connected with the child's "needs for physical care, nourishment, comfort, affection and stimulation. Only a parent who provides for these needs will build a psychological relationship to the child—and will become his 'psychological parent' in whose care the child will feel valued and 'wanted'" (p. 17).

Through these close relationships, the child acquires and internalizes parental attitudes and expectations. These identifications are the core of each child's unique personality. It is essential to remember that "so long as the child is part of a viable family, his own interests are merged with those of other family members. Only *after* the family fails in its function should the child's interests become a matter for state intrusion" (Goldstein, Freud, and Solnit 1979, title page).

In child-placement conflicts, through statute or case law, the principle of "the best interests of the child" is the prevailing standard in the United States. However, there often is disagreement as to the specific meaning of "best interests." As conceptualized by Goldstein, Freud, and Solnit (1979, 4–14), the issue can be clarified if, in formulating priorities for children and adults, we are guided by two value preferences: first, that intrusion by the state into the privacy of a family should be minimal; and second, that when a child's best interests conflict with fairness for the interested adults, the child's best interests shall be paramount.

Children's rights are those privileges and assurances guaranteed to them by societal agreement either through custom or through law. Children's needs—for affectionate care, protection, and guidance—are met by adults who have learned the caretaking role via intuition, earlier experience, or training. Clearly, children need the insulating, protecting, decision-making authority of nurturing parents who do not abandon them to their "rights." There is a shift in needs, capacities, and tolerances along the developmental continuum from infancy to adolescence as the individual child moves from relative helplessness and dependency to an increasing capacity for self-starting initiative and independence. Once children reach adulthood, they are assumed to be capable of taking their own risks.

Children's rights, especially in the younger years, thus are subsumed under their need for the constancy of caretaking adults, usually their biological parents, who become their psychological parents. The parents will determine how their children's needs can best be met in the context of a family with a unique historical or cultural background whose overall integrity is assured by the parents' relative autonomy. Paradoxically, while asserting their rights to provide for their children's need for affectionate care and continuity, parents may, on the basis of religious, ethical, or philosophical beliefs, for example, refuse to allow the state to immunize their children. This apparent contradiction between the child's needs and rights must be clarified to make sure that parents who decline the state's services will accept other useful ways to provide children with the help they need.

Our view brings children's rights and needs into a harmonious relationship by indicating what is most important for children and how needs and rights evolve over time from infancy to adolescence. If parents are disqualified or disqualify themselves from taking care of their children, however, the state as *parens patriae* must intervene to guarantee to children the rights that our society has implicitly or explicitly granted them.

As stated in *Before the Best Interests of the Child* (Goldstein, Freud, and Solnit 1979, 4–5):

> First, we believe that a child's need for continuity of care by autonomous parents requires acknowledging that parents should generally be entitled to raise their children as they think best, free of state interference. . . . Second, we believe that the child's well-being . . . must be determinative once justification for state intervention has been established. . . . The goal of intervention must be to create or recreate a family for the child as quickly as possible. That conviction is expressed in our preference for *making a child's interests paramount.*

The goal of every child placement, be it by birth or by court order, is to assure that the child is a member of a functioning family, "a family with at least one parent [or parent substitute] who wants him. It is to assure for each child and his parents an opportunity to maintain, establish or reestablish psychological ties to each other free of further interruption by the state" (Goldstein, Freud, and Solnit 1979, 5).

In the same book, Goldstein, Freud, and Solnit (1979, 6) state the following principles for determining placement of children whose custody becomes the subject of legal action:

> Placement decisions should safeguard the child's need for continuity of relationships.

Placement decisions should reflect the child's, not the
adult's, sense of time.*

Placement decisions must take into account the law's incapacity to supervise interpersonal relationships and the limits
of our knowledge to make long-range predictions.

The authors remind us that by the time the state has inter-
vened, a child's development may already have been jeopardized
by neglect, abandonment, or abuse. The opportunity to provide
an ideal environment has passed. To minimize the damage to a
child's growth and development, the caseworker often must search
for what the authors term "the least detrimental alternative."

Continuity—of relationships, surroundings, and environmental influences—is essential for children. Our conviction of this is
based on our understanding of how emotional attachments in early
life form the bedrock of subsequent attachments. For these relationships to be internalized and elaborated, the child needs the
stability that is reflected in external continuity and permanency.
Disruptions in continuity can have various consequences, depending on the age of the child. From birth to about 18 months,
even a shift in routine may cause discomfort, but the most serious
effect on the emotional development of infants and toddlers results
from a change of the primary caretaking person. When separated
from a familiar adult, young children suffer not only distress but
also setbacks in the quality of their ensuing attachments. Research
and clinical experience, however, have shown that subsequent attachments to new caretakers may reach previous levels of trust-
fulness and enrichment, reflecting infants' intense needs for adults
who will love and take care of them. Nevertheless, multiple placements in the early years may lead to increasingly shallow and in-
discriminate attachments (Goldstein, Freud, and Solnit 1979).

*"Unlike adults . . . children have their own built-in time sense [which]
results in their marked intolerance for postponement of gratification or frustration, and an intense sensitivity to the length of separations" (Goldstein,
Freud, and Solnit 1973, 11).

Until a child is about 5, disruptions of continuity with a stable parent figure also may affect such early accomplishments as speech and toilet training. With school-age children, breaks in relationships with their psychological parents may affect achievements that are based on identifications with the parents' demands, prohibitions, and social ideals. Such identifications develop where attachments are consistent and predictable; children who must move from one environment to another often fail to achieve the level of identification with loving adults that is so essential for healthy development. Resentful toward the adults who have disappointed them, children sometimes respond defensively by pretending not to care; others destructively test or scapegoat the new parents for the shortcomings of those who preceded them.

Continuity of attachments is no less important for adolescents, despite the impression created by their developmentally expected revolt against parental authority. Like younger children, adolescents need the stability of external arrangements.

The child's sense of time, based on the urgency of his or her instinctual needs, is another important consideration underlying the concept of the "least detrimental alternative" (Goldstein, Freud, and Solnit 1979). For the child, the significance of separations depends on their duration and frequency and on the developmental period in which they occur. How long it takes to break an old attachment or to form a new one will depend on a variety of factors, including the different meanings time holds for children at various ages.

Each child's unique makeup, of course, indicates which of many factors will be crucial in determining the quality of his or her attachments, their strengths and weaknesses, in good times and bad. As an infant's memory becomes a reliable source for anticipating how frustrations, wishes, and needs are endured, gratified, and relieved, the child gradually develops the capacity to delay gratifications and to anticipate the future.

An infant or toddler often feels overwhelmed, after a few days, by the departure of a parent or parents. The presence of new psychological parents, however quickly the child appears to accept them, may not completely heal the injury incurred by a loss sustained earlier. As a practical guide, for most children between the ages of 2 and 5 a separation from familiar caretakers of more than two months is upsetting to a degree that may lead to significant psychological harm, especially if the temporary caretakers are strangers. The younger school-age child may similarly experience an absence of six months, as an older child would an absence of a year or more, especially if evidence of parental concern and expectations is lacking.

This sense-of-time principle suggests that if anyone is to be kept waiting in placement decisions, it should not be the child, whose capacity to endure loss or uncertainty should not be exceeded. Quick action by decision makers increases the chance of restoring stability to an existing parent-child relationship or facilitating the establishment of a new one.

Finally, the child's need to feel wanted is the third component of the principle of best interests and perhaps the most essential criterion in placing the child. Only a child who has at least one individual to love and be loved by will acquire a healthy self-esteem and the likelihood of a progressive development. The determination of who that individual is often poses difficulties. The adult best suited for this role is the one with whom the child has had and continues to have an affectionate bond. The younger the child and the longer the period of separation or uncertainty, the more urgent is the need, "even without perfect knowledge," to place the child quickly and permanently.

These principles of child development suggest that laws of child placement should minimize unwarranted intrusions into family integrity. Goldstein, Freud, and Solnit (1979) propose grounds for state intervention that seek to incorporate the standard of the least detrimental alternative with a preference for minimal state intrusion:

1. Reported abuse, neglect, or abandonment of a child.

2. The death or disappearance of both parents, the only parent, or the custodial parent coupled with failure to make provision for the child's custody and care.

3. A parent's request that the state place the child.

4. The request by a child's long-time caretakers to become his parents or the refusal by long-time caretakers to relinquish a child to his parents or to a state agency.

5. The parents' refusal to authorize life-saving medical care for the child.

3

The Caseworker's Role

The task of the Protective Services worker involves three processes: inquiry, assessment, and decision making. On the basis of a report or a request for help, he or she initially investigates complaints of neglect, abuse, and risk of injury. Having obtained whatever facts are available, the worker then attempts to assess the risk to the child and to determine the needs of the family and its capacity to function. He or she then assesses the family's ability to use existing services in the community. Once the facts have been ascertained and the assessments made, the worker decides whether to provide services that will enable the child to remain safely in the family or to place him or her outside the home. The provision of specific services is intended to eliminate or minimize the factor of specific risk.

After the decision to place has been made, other difficult questions arise. These include whether the placement should occur on a "voluntary"* basis or by court order, how long the child should endure the uncertainty of placement, and what decision should be made for a permanent plan.

The worker's decision will be based not only on the factors already mentioned but also on an understanding of his or her role and a knowledge of child development acquired through education and training. This knowledge informs such concepts, for example, as that of permanency. The goal of permanency, which assures stabilization and continuity for the child, requires the worker to gather data immediately toward a plan for the child's return home or continuation in placement outside the original home—either

*The word "voluntary" here appears in quotation marks because once the state becomes responsible for the care of a child, parents give up part of their autonomy and do not have the right to regain their child without permission of the state.

through adoption, transfer of guardianship, or permanent foster care. Only a worker who is knowledgeable about the developing child's need for continuity of love, the predictability of care, and the stability of parental figures will be capable of individual case management in keeping with these concepts.

The worker's clear understanding of his or her role and its limits can be assured through continuing clinical experience, supervision, consultation, and selected opportunities to keep abreast with the field through participation in seminars, conferences, lectures, and other postgraduate learning experiences. As professionals, workers strive to make decisions that are as free from personal bias as possible. This can be difficult as they are constantly confronted by issues that ordinarily arouse feelings of moral outrage and condemnation. Workers learn to develop judgment without becoming judgmental and to inform and sometimes confront parents without becoming punitive. Experienced workers and supervisors acquire self-knowledge and use this knowledge, together with training, to reduce the undesirable effects of their personal biases.

One of the hardest tasks for a new worker is becoming reconciled to the inherent contradictions in the Protective Services worker's role. The worker is expected to aim for two goals, which in some instances may be mutually exclusive: reunification of the family, and protection of the child and the child's best interests. The worker is, above all, responsible for decisions concerning the child's safety, but in the complex attempt to clarify and resolve placement issues, other factors—such as the quality of relationships that have been formed in the past or in the newly constituted family—also must be considered. In practice, therefore, the determination of a plan that will serve the child's best interests may not lead to reunification with his or her biological family. Supervision and consultation help the worker to focus on the individual child and to construct a therapeutic plan appropriate to the child's needs.

Another key element in decision making is the worker's ability to assess a family's service needs. Such an ability is acquired through supervision and the assistance of expert evaluation when the worker determines it to be necessary.

Supervision and consultation are specific sources of support that should be available on a regular basis. Supervision can be defined as a process in which two people participate in a joint effort to establish and maintain or elevate a level of performance. The supervisor uses empathy and his or her knowledge of theory and practice to assist the worker in dealing with the intricacies of a difficult case.

The supervisor activates the worker's potential, thereby supporting his or her skill and development. The complexity of human behavior and the myriad issues of theory, practice, and policy are interpreted to workers by the supervisor for application to individual cases. Although workers must immerse themselves in the details of their cases in order to gain specific knowledge about particular children and their families, it is often the help of the supervisor that makes it possible to view a case in perspective. A good case plan, which results from the interaction of supervisor and worker, will take into account the principles of child development that have been cited earlier—that is, the child's sense of time, need for continuity of relationships, and need to be wanted by at least one psychological parent.

Given the complexity inherent in decision making, it is important that the worker, in collaboration with the supervisor, also recognize situations in which specific problems require consultation with one or more experts outside the agency, such as a child development expert, clinical social worker, neurologist, pediatrician, psychiatrist, psychoanalyst, psychologist, or public health nurse. In seeking consultation, the supervisor and the worker should formulate the questions that they wish the consultant to address for the purpose of clarifying specific issues.

Another source of support for the worker is collaboration with other agencies. Meeting with associates in other fields facilitates the discussion of problems and possible solutions and the sharing of frustrations and can also foster a sense of teamwork. Child abuse and neglect need to be viewed in a community setting and require collaboration of workers with other institutions, such as boards of education, social work agencies, child guidance clinics, welfare departments, and youth service bureaus. Taking on the challenge of these difficult problems in our society requires a collective effort.

The worker needs to have a knowledge of the services available in the family's community, the ability to help the family obtain the services, and the capacity to coordinate them. The worker should distinguish between two types of referral or consultation. One is intended to help Child Protective Services (CPS) workers formulate a service plan. Such a consultation with another agency usually is not confidential. The second type of referral is for counseling or psychiatric treatment. In this situation the worker should respect and make every effort to protect the family's right to confidentiality.

As already mentioned, the job of child protection can be associated with tremendous stress, and vocational hazards abound. When dealing with issues of separation, termination of parental rights, and placement, workers sometimes experience apprehension, guilt, and despair. Furthermore, finding "good" foster homes or adequate placement facilities is often difficult, especially in emergency situations.

In practice, effective workers become comfortable with their authority without becoming authoritarian. They resist internal pressures to identify either with the helplessness of the children whom they serve or with the aggression of some of the parents with whom they work. Through experience and the continuing training involved in supervision and consultation, they develop the capacity to cope with a child's painful experience of loss or shattering disappointment in the face of a parent's rejection or abandonment. Workers learn to identify the viable alternatives available for the child and to accept the least detrimental alternative as the most realistic one.

Workers must endure the devastation of the child who is injured by caretakers. When a child is killed or permanently injured by an adult, workers confronted by their inability to prevent such an event are at risk of becoming overwhelmed by feelings of sadness and helplessness. Powerful psychological issues are constantly alive in child protection work and are taxing to those who confront them on a daily basis. For this reason, workers need knowledgeable, supportive supervision and stimulation toward professional growth as they take on some of our society's formidable problems.

4

Illustrative
Cases

I f a child has been physically . . . assaulted (so that the child's life or physical safety is threatened), the presumption is that the child must be assured of being in a safer environment." Assuring a "safer environment" usually implies removing the child from the home, removing the abuser from the home, or introducing services that will ensure the child's safety if he or she remains at home.*

Children Who Are Removed from Home

Emergency or Immediate Removal

Emergency or immediate removal is an infrequent procedure. When immediate physical danger to a child is overwhelmingly likely, it generally is anticipated, and a planned removal is put into effect. Cases 1 through 4, however, were situations that necessitated emergency or immediate removal.

CASE 1

Sarita and Lester. Life-threatening injuries sustained by children at hands of mother. Co-terminous petition filed.†

Following life-threatening injuries to Sarita, age 27 months, and Lester, 10 months, a co-terminous petition was filed by CPS and contested by Mr. and Mrs. Bartlett, the parents. An evaluation was requested to help the court determine whether to proceed with the termination of parental rights or whether the children could be returned safely to their parents.

Mrs. Bartlett, aged 26, had had recurrent periods of depression

*See appendix 1. These cases are organized according to the Connecticut Guidelines.

†Co-terminous refers to the simultaneous request for commitment of children to the state's custody and termination of parental rights. Co-terminous decisions are discussed more fully in chapter 5.

since adolescence. First pregnant at 16 (by Mr. Bartlett, whom she later married), she ran away from home and had an abortion. Her second child, born with a birth defect, lived for three weeks. She subsequently had a year-long affair with her husband's brother, which temporarily broke up the marriage; during this time she made a suicide attempt. Sarita and Lester were born after the marriage resumed. Mrs. Bartlett discontinued her therapy with a private psychiatrist the year before the events recounted here.

After giving her children and herself doses of Valium and whiskey, Mrs. Bartlett severely lacerated her children's wrists as well as her own. Mr. Bartlett, who had observed the beginnings of his wife's psychotic behavior, including finding her in the bathroom with a knife, nevertheless left the house for several hours to go bowling. Upon returning home to find his now-injured family, he called an ambulance. The children had successful surgical repairs of their wounds. Following a week's hospitalization, they were discharged to a paternal aunt, who was able to offer them only temporary care. As Mrs. Bartlett was due to be released from a mental hospital and was deemed to pose a potential threat to the safety of the children if they were returned home, the CPS worker decided to obtain an Order of Temporary Custody and place the children in foster care.

Mr. and Mrs. Bartlett very much wanted to regain custody of their children. They embarked on weekly marital counseling, and Mrs. Bartlett also was seen in individual psychotherapy. The worker decided to file a co-terminous petition, and a court-ordered evaluation was undertaken by a child psychiatrist. During the evaluation, Mrs. Bartlett revealed that prior to her attempts on her children's lives she had become convinced that her husband was Jesus and that she was God's daughter; this delusion was succeeded by the opposite notion, that the devil had possessed her and would possess her children. Believing that a nuclear war was imminent, she had decided to kill her children and then herself to spare them all prolonged suffering.

Mrs. Bartlett was observed to have real affection and concern for her children, stated her distress at having believed "those stupid, crazy ideas," and expressed anxiety about the impact of her attack on them. Mr. Bartlett, who acknowledged his former lack of involvement with his wife and children, now claimed that he loved his wife and that the children were needed at home to help her get better. He feared, according to the CPS worker's report, that if the children were not returned, their mother would "have too much time on her hands and [would] become a selfish person."

The child psychiatrist, basing his evaluation on interviews with the parents and the children singly and together, ended his study with this statement:

> I recommend to the Court that, despite the strong, ongoing positive psychological bonds between parents and children, and despite Mr. and Mrs. Bartlett's hard work to remedy the problems that led to the murder-suicide attempt, Sarita and Lester should never be returned to Mr. and Mrs. Bartlett's custody. Mrs. Bartlett's past psychiatric history and the savageness of her suicide-murder attempt dictate that the children can never be truly safe with their mother. Sarita and Lester should be placed as expeditiously as possible in a permanent loving home so that they can begin to form attachments to new psychological parents.

Considerations in this case:

1. The worker decided on immediate removal of the children when the father "chose" his wife instead of his children. His decision to allow his wife to return home after her murderous actions revealed his inability to provide a safe environment.

2. Despite the strength of the psychological bonds between parents and children and the parents' supposed recognition of their problems, the evaluation by the child psychiatrist documented this clear example of life-threatening abuse, which warranted the children's removal from their home forever.

3. There was no evidence that these parents, either alone or together, could provide a safe environment for the children.

Follow-up:

Sarita and Lester were committed to the state and placed in foster care immediately after the findings of abuse were substantiated. Because of due process, however, their mother's parental rights were not terminated until eighteen months after her attack on them; her appeal was denied by the Connecticut Supreme Court one year later. At this time, following two favorable CPS home studies of the father, Sarita, now 4 years and 9 months old, and Lester, aged 3, were returned to him. Mr. Bartlett, having divorced his wife, from then on assumed sole parental and house-keeping responsibility for his children. He agreed that Mrs. Bartlett should have no access to the children and that any contact between them could jeopardize their safety.

Two and a half years after the children were returned to him, Mr. Bartlett filed a petition for revocation of the Order of Commitment to the state,* which was granted. He had proven capable of meeting his children's needs. He evidently had a warm relationship with both his daughter and his son, who according to school and pediatric accounts were thriving. His job of six years' duration provided sufficient income to pay for after-school day-care services.

Comment:

Although the clinical evaluation previously obtained was valid, this case indicates the limitations of our ability to make long-term predictions. Two years after the children were placed in foster care, an evaluation of the father revealed that he had rehabilitated himself and was competent to care for his children. He was able to build on his earlier relationship with them, exploiting the "strong

---

*In Connecticut, the Order of Commitment to the state refers to a court-ordered placement of the child with the state as custodial parent.

. . . positive psychological bonds" with them that previously had been noted.

CASE 2

Joan. Firstborn infant with life-threatening injuries inflicted by one or both parents. Co-terminous petition filed following an Order of Temporary Custody.

As an instance of emergency removal the case of Joan Truslow exemplifies teamwork between CPS workers and other professionals.

Joan Truslow was the subject of a co-terminous petition filed by CPS when, at the age of 4 months, she was hospitalized with new or healing fractures of both legs, one upper arm, and eight ribs. After ruling out osteogenesis imperfecta,* several physicians agreed that her injuries could have resulted only from forceful trauma induced by shaking and twisting. Two bites, showing the marks of human teeth, also were noted on her shoulder and back.

Joan had been seen twice previously by her pediatrician, at age 6 weeks with a lacerated lip, and at 3 months with black eyes and a bruised nose. On these occasions the parents had attributed the injuries, respectively, to the infant's having scratched herself with her fingernail and to her having toppled from her infant seat. Neither explanation was thought to be credible. The only explanation the parents could offer for the fractures was that they had occurred at birth.

Upon Joan's discharge from the hospital two weeks later, CPS obtained an Order of Temporary Custody and placed her in a foster home. When just over 6 months old, in response to a court order, she was given a developmental evaluation by a child psychiatrist who also interviewed her parents. The infant's examination was remarkable in that she was found to be about seven

*Osteogenesis imperfecta is an inherited condition in which the bones are abnormally brittle and susceptible to fractures from impacts that ordinarily would not cause injuries.

weeks delayed in her development. According to assessments by both the foster mother and the pediatrician, her developmental delay had been even more severe when she entered foster care seven weeks earlier.

A noteworthy aspect of this case was the behavior of Joan's parents. Both Mr. and Mrs. Truslow, ages 27 and 18 respectively, although apparently well oriented and showing no evidence of thought or process disorders, adamantly denied knowing the cause of Joan's injuries, while simultaneously insisting that they had been their daughter's sole caretakers. This bizarre point was reemphasized in court in testimony by the child psychiatrist and a social worker. "In [the former's] experience of child abuse he found it 'very unusual' that Joan's parents were so consistent in maintaining that the baby had been in the mother's sole care at all times but that they could not imagine how any of the injuries had occurred." Mrs. Truslow also minimized the importance of Joan's developmental delays. On the basis of his evaluation of Joan, the child psychiatrist recommended that she "never again be placed with her parents because of the unremitting child abuse and that she be placed for adoption as expeditiously as possible."

When Joan was 15 months old (at least ten months after her discharge from the hospital), the rights of her parents were terminated after a four-day court trial by a judge of a Superior Court for Juvenile Matters. This decision was expressed in an eloquent memorandum, which cited the child psychiatrist as "the most compelling witness." The memorandum quoted the respondent parents as relying on a section of a state of Connecticut bulletin that stated a general preference for all children to grow up in their natural homes. "What was not cited," the memorandum continued, "was [another important] portion of the policy found in that bulletin." The judge here quoted the co-terminous paragraph from the Guidelines.*

*Bulletin #30 from Connecticut's *Manual Volume 2* of the Division of Protective Services. See appendix 1.

The case of Joan Truslow did not end with this judge's pronouncement, however. Her parents filed their intention to appeal the decision and subsequently won the right for weekly visitation with their daughter at a CPS office. In the meantime, Joan had been placed in an adoptive home. The adoptive parents were aware of the appeal and of the legal risk involved in accepting Joan for placement.

When the child was 21 months old, in connection with the judge's request for an in-court review of the status of this case, the CPS worker expressed concern to the child psychiatrist about visits to Joan by the biological parents. A successor CPS worker, entering the case when Joan was 2½ years old, was even more apprehensive. She was persuaded that the visits by the parents might weaken and confuse the child's excellent relationship with her prospective adoptive family and that, with increasing age, the child might inadvertently disclose to the biological parents the identity or whereabouts of her new family. The biological parents had recently pleaded guilty to risk of injury, and Mrs. Truslow was sentenced to imprisonment for up to three years. But visitation with the father, who had been placed on probation for five years, continued.

When Joan was 32 months old the same child psychiatrist, at the request of CPS, again performed an evaluation, this time with the impact of visitation as its subject. The psychiatrist wrote:

> During the course of her legal-risk adoptive placement Joan formed a strong, warm and trusting relationship with her legal-risk adoptive parents. . . . Despite the history and despite termination of parental rights . . . more than 1½ years have passed since the co-terminous petition was decided and Joan's placement has still not been made secure. . . . She has now reached a stage . . . where her language and cognitive skills will cause her to be much more vulnerable to anxiety and confusion about visits with her

biological parents. In addition the continued visitation is causing considerable stress to her caretakers and is disrupting their sense of confidence in the permanency of Joan's placement with them. . . .

Joan's ability to grow up in a safe and secure environment has already been jeopardized by her biological parents' assault . . . and is again being jeopardized. . . . I strongly recommend to the court that Joan not be subjected to further visitation with her biological parents and that the finalization of her adoption be completed as soon as possible.

The final chapter came early in Joan's fourth year. In response to the biological parents' appeal to the Connecticut Supreme Court, in which they sought to overturn the decision of the original judge because of technical errors, the higher court upheld the ruling of the Superior Court. Visitation rights were discontinued, and Joan was adopted legally at last.

Considerations in this case:

1. The CPS worker filed the co-terminous petition based on the severe fractures sustained by a 4-month-old infant. The worker was not diverted by the parents' persistent and strenuous denial of any knowledge of the child's injury.

2. The child's sense of time was ignored. Due process and appeals were carried out solely according to the adults' sense of time, from the child's fourth month of age through her fourth year. The failure to recognize a young child's sense of time is detrimental because children under the age of 8 or 9 are unable to tolerate not knowing who will love and safeguard them. A further complication was the long delay, which slowed down and jeopardized the formation of a primary relationship between the child and the adoptive parents.

(Note: It later was learned that the father had been the abuser and that the mother had protected him. From the child's point of view, it little matters whether the parent abuses or permits the abuse. In either case, removal of the child under such circumstances is lifesaving.)

CASE 3

Susan. Suspiciously injured infant of a mother who previously had injured an older child.

In this case an emergency removal was carried out after a dangerous delay.

Susan Wolensky, age 4½ months, was brought to the hospital by her pleasant, well-spoken 21-year-old single mother, who stated that when she had pulled the baby to a sitting position, Susan's left arm "popped" and she no longer could move it. The child was examined and discharged as being in good condition by the emergency room physician. Later the same day, ostensibly worried by Susan's crying, Ms. Wolensky returned to the hospital, where X-rays were taken. These revealed several-week-old fractures of Susan's right arm and also of her right seventh rib. The same emergency room physician believed that these injuries could have been sustained accidentally if Ms. Wolensky, as she reported, had twice dropped the baby. She said that on one occasion she had become dizzy, "blacked out," and perhaps fallen on the baby. Ms. Wolensky suggested that on another occasion, Susan might have fallen against the side of her crib. The following day, Susan's pediatrician informed the emergency room physician that Susan's 6-year-old half-brother had suffered a fractured femur at the age of 2 weeks, and at 2 months had sustained an intracranial hemorrhage, which left him severely and irreparably brain damaged.

As a result of this new information, CPS was notified, and a home visit was made that day. The worker took a brief family history and observed that the mother handled the baby carelessly. She noted that "mother does not seem to be aware of the fragility of the infant." No substantive action resulted from this meeting. The worker noted the mother's explanation of her second hospital visit of the day before ("It's better to be safe than sorry"), referred her to a parent enrichment program, and planned to meet with her further.

On learning of this case, the program supervisor and a clinical consultant concluded that additional exploration was warranted. Accordingly, they arranged a case conference with a consultant pediatrician. This pediatrician, upon review of the medical records, stated that the X-rays of Susan's old fractures belied the mother's story of how the injuries had occurred. He felt that only "a considerable blow" could have caused them.

This physician's opinion of the inadequacy of the mother's explanation, together with the history of Ms. Wolensky's first child, provided sufficient grounds to remove Susan from her mother immediately—an intervention that may well have saved the baby from subsequent injuries. The difficulty of this assignment for the social worker should be noted. Having gained the trust of Ms. Wolensky, the worker was then obliged to inform her of, and expedite, the plan for Susan's immediate removal.

In this instance a realistic appraisal of Susan's situation, based not only on her injuries but also on the previous histories of both mother and sibling, could have indicated the "overwhelming likelihood of immediate physical danger to the child." The opinion of the consulting physician left no doubt that this child was in jeopardy.

Considerations in this case:

1. The extent of the baby's injuries initially was denied by her mother, hospital personnel, and a CPS intake worker.

2. Overcoming a caretaker's denial of abuse requires a sustained questioning attitude, as well as collaboration with colleagues. In this instance, the additional history of a previous life-threatening injury to an older child was significant. (It should be noted that such a history in itself would not be cause for removal.)

Follow-up:

Ms. Wolensky's parental rights were terminated when Susan was 16 months old. The child was placed with a family who adopted her at age 2½. (Two years after Susan was born, Ms. Wolensky gave birth to a third child, a boy, who suffered a skull fracture during his second month. He recovered. Long-term custody of this child was transferred to the paternal grandmother, with no plan for return to the mother. Ms. Wolensky has been satisfied by brief weekly visits with the child, supervised by the grandmother.)

Discussion:

Parents who abuse their children often deny the injuries in order to ward off criticism, guilt, and legal censure. A strong tendency also exists for adults to deny the fact that parents are capable of harming their own children. Adults tend to identify with other adults rather than with the helpless child.

The blind spots that here affected both a young physician in the hospital emergency room and an intake worker should be noted. Each professional needs to be aware of his or her personal bias, which is often in favor of individuals with whom they can identify. Although professionals are expected to be able to form a working alliance with all parents, they must nonetheless correct for bias that hinders their ability to make an accurate diagnosis or to recognize the realities of an injury. We are more likely to want to believe individuals who appear to be cooperative, compliant, and well-spoken than those who seem belligerent, suspicious, and inarticulate.

CASE 4

Sophia. Child with congenital defect and series of injuries.

"An exception to removing the child may be warranted when . . . (a) Assessment is adequate to identify the factors that caused the abuse and . . . (b) There are sufficient services to reduce significantly the risk of remaining in the home."* This case illustrates a quandary in which a worker often is caught: at what point should a child be removed from the home? In this instance, an abused child was not removed in time to spare her serious injury.

*See appendix 1.

Mrs. Belsky, aged 24, had a long history of drug and alcohol abuse. When four months pregnant with her second child, Sophia, she was hospitalized following an overdose of alcohol, methadone, and Valium. She had been taking both Valium and methadone when she gave birth to Sophia. The baby was born with a cleft palate and other oral anomalies and spent her first eleven months in the hospital. Initially, hospital staff contacted CPS when Mrs. Belsky's infrequent visits to the baby led to the fear that she had abandoned her. Toward the end of the hospitalization, however, with staff encouragement she stayed with the baby for a week to learn how to care for her.

A second referral was made to CPS when Sophia was 2 years old, following a routine medical evaluation that revealed bruises and the imprint of a hand on the child. The worker's anxiety was now aroused, and many home services were marshaled to ensure the child's well-being. Nonetheless, a month later she suffered a spiral fracture of the right femur and eight months later still, a burn on her ear, for which she was again hospitalized.

Despite Sophia's injuries from abuse and Mrs. Belsky's acknowledgment of her continued use of heroin and other drugs, the child was not placed in foster care until after her second hospitalization. With unrecognized ambivalence and massive guilt, Mrs. Belsky, helped by her mother, contracted with CPS to facilitate Sophia's return home. Within two months this request was granted, and the mother again was provided with a wide variety of services in the evident belief that these services would counteract any threat she might pose to her daughter's safety.

One might speculate that the CPS worker had become so emotionally involved in this case that she identified and formed a friendship with the likable mother, thereby losing sight of her professional role and function. This again underscores how difficult it is for professionals to sustain their identification with young children. Eight months after her return home, Sophia was hospitalized with third-degree burns on about 35 percent of her body and other serious injuries, including further fractures. Mrs. Belsky could remember only that she had been drinking heavily, that her daughter had burned herself on a space heater, and that she had hit Sophia before passing out.

Sophia in time recovered and was adopted by a nurturing family after her mother had voluntarily terminated her parental rights. Mrs. Belsky served a prison sentence and was released on parole. To determine whether she would be able to provide a stable home for her three remaining children, who were placed in foster care at the time of her incarceration, CPS requested a consultation (see Case 11). This included both psychiatric and psychological evaluations and five in-depth interviews conducted by the clinical consultant. The accumulated information not only provided the consultant with a basis for her recommendation but also shed much light on the underlying factors of Mrs. Belsky's pernicious behavior toward her second child. A partial summary follows:

> This is a complex case, in which Mrs. Belsky's incapacity to parent Sophia and the professionals' failure to respond adequately to abuse almost resulted in Sophia's death. Mrs. Belsky was unable to take care of Sophia because of the particular meaning her birth defect had for her. She experienced her daughter's defectiveness as both a punishment to her for her own "badness" and as a visible . . . exposure of the part of herself she viewed pejoratively. . . . Her feelings about herself were rooted in earlier experiences of childhood, including her inability to think of herself as having value and her chronic exposure to violence. . . . She saw Sophia as the worst of herself and could no more take care of her than she had been able to take care of herself. . . . As far as is known, Mrs. Belsky's destructive behavior was directed only toward Sophia.

Had the worker given sufficient weight to the child's continuing injuries despite services, Sophia probably would have been removed from the home before the almost-fatal final injury—which necessitated an emergency removal. Before that tragic episode, the worker had believed, or wished to believe, that providing services to the parent would be sufficient to assure the child of a "safer environment." Yet a more important factor was overlooked: the cause of the abuse was not identified adequately until long after the victim had been removed to safety. Although a good deal of planning and careful supervision was involved, sound principles were followed in returning her three other children to Mrs. Belsky's care after her release from prison.

Considerations in this case:

1. The mother's behavior toward her defective child from birth on was not understood. During the baby's earliest months in the hospital, the mother-child relationship should have been evaluated by an expert. Such an evaluation would have revealed whether services could be effective or whether the mother was indicating the limits of her ability to love and care for her defective child.

2. Once the child was at home in the mother's care, a pattern of repeated abuse was overlooked. Following the fracture of the child's arm, for example, an emergency removal from the home would have been warranted. After all, this fracture occurred in the context of a series of injuries and a highly charged mother-child relationship.

3. Many of the professionals in the case were themselves unable to tolerate this mother's rejection of her defective child. They ignored her feelings and encouraged her to take on a task she could not perform. Crucial indicators, such as the injuries and the mother's significant abuse of alcohol and of drugs, were ignored.

4. Siblings (see Case 11).

Planned Removal (planned over several days, weeks, or months)
CASE 5
Samuel. Infant with substance-abusing mother.

Whereas the four previous cases immediately or ultimately resulted in emergency removals, that of Samuel Wolf, born to a drug-addicted mother, raised the question of whether the infant was at imminent risk and therefore a candidate for placement from the hospital. Imminent risk is "a situation in which the behavior of the adult caretakers, whether by omission or commission, threatens serious damage to the child or endangers the child's life."*

When Samuel was born, hospital authorities notified CPS that his 30-year-old mother was a drug addict. She freely admitted taking heroin and street methadone daily, plus a pint of vodka. Her two older children, one of whom was addicted at birth, were being raised by aunts. However, there was no evidence that Samuel was addicted.

Since Ms. Wolf had no home and neither the physical nor the financial resources to meet the infant's needs, she "voluntarily"† consented to his temporary foster placement. She signed a contract in which she agreed to undertake certain tasks during this time. Although she told the CPS worker that she wanted Samuel with her and the chance to make up for past mistakes, her actions in no way bore this out. In fact, she abandoned the baby.

Samuel was first hospitalized at 1 month of age with seizures and again soon after, with an intestinal disorder from which he nearly died. His mother's lack of interest was marked. She scarcely visited him during his hospital stays; only with difficulty could she be located to sign essential forms. More often than not she sounded incoherent or appeared to be intoxicated. Neither she nor Samuel's father was available to discuss their son's medical needs or specialized post-hospital care, and they did not maintain contact with either the foster mother or the CPS worker. Not surprisingly, Ms. Wolf also broke the terms of the signed contract, which included arranging for housing and entering a drug rehabilitation program. The foster mother was an affectionate person who often

*Appendix 1.
†See footnote on p. 21.

visited the hospital up to three times daily and, upon the baby's release, meticulously attended to his difficult feeding needs (which included weighing ingredients for his formula on a special scale). Samuel appeared to be thriving in her care.

A prodigious amount of work was performed by CPS for six months in an effort to understand and improve Samuel's situation: meetings with parents, grandmother, aunts, uncles, medical personnel, and foster family; innumerable letters and telephone calls; extensive research into the native American background of both parents for purposes of subsequent placement (which proved to be futile); arrangements for a developmental examination of the baby and psychological examinations of both his parents.

When Samuel was 6 months old, the CPS evaluation and plan, as submitted to the court, ended as follows: "Samuel's parents . . . are both presently incarcerated. . . . It is felt that it is not in the child's best interest to postpone termination proceedings. . . . It is recommended . . . that Samuel be free for adoption by his foster mother, if possible."

Considerations in this case:

1. This case illustrates the advantages to the child of a petition filed in record time and the efficient pursuit by the worker of all options leading to permanent placement.

2. The process of inquiry, assessment, and decision making preceded planned removal. This child had been abandoned. To return him to his home was impossible because of the imminent risk of physical damage due to severe neglect. His parents did not want him.

CASE 6

Juanita. Removal and termination of parental rights in unusual instance of neglect. Services offered.

The case of Juanita Hogan provides another example of planned removal from the home, the unusual circumstances that necessitated it, and the painstaking methods that led to this decision.

Juanita, a healthy full-term biracial baby, was born to a 40-year-old woman who was unaware of her pregnancy until the eighth month. All that was known of the father was that he was black. Mrs. Hogan's behavior following delivery, plus her long history of mental illness, troubled hospital staff members, who made contact with CPS. A program of intensive home services was initiated, which included three visits a week by a CPS worker and four visits a week of three hours each by a parent aide. In her first year of life, Juanita appeared to progress well; her early developmental landmarks were within normal limits. During this time, however, the various providers of support services became increasingly concerned about Mrs. Hogan's lack of affect and inability to offer appropriate stimulation to the baby.

The living situation was marginal. Juanita and Mrs. Hogan shared a bed in a hotel room. Their kitchen facilities consisted of a refrigerator and a hot plate, from which the baby once suffered a burn. Juanita slept about fifteen hours out of twenty-four; her only "toy" was a teething ring. Mrs. Hogan rarely went out and had no friends, no telephone, and no television. Juanita did not have any opportunity to socialize with other children.

The CPS worker referred Juanita at 16 months to a child guidance clinic. The evaluator found her to be unusually passive and withdrawn. Although her abilities were difficult to assess, they were thought to be age-appropriate, with the exception of delayed language development, assessed at about the 9-month level. The examiner attributed this delay to the child's environmental deprivation and termed her to be at high risk for retarded development. Several months later, Juanita was enrolled in a four-day-per-week preschool program. Unfortunately, the various home support services were discontinued at about this time.

When Juanita was 22 months old, her teacher, though reporting improvement in such areas as peer relationships, expressed definite concerns about the child's well-being. Her lack of speech was striking, as was her refusal to eat in the presence of others. She showed no emotion at all when separating from her mother. Juanita was unkempt and dirty, with clothes often unsuited to the weather.

At the behest of CPS, when Juanita was 28 months old a clinical expert gave her another developmental examination and also met with her mother. This examiner found Juanita's inherent endowment to be within the average range but noted that "severe delays and distortions in her speech, social and emotional development reveal the adverse effect on her of her mother's handicap. Mrs. Hogan's behavior reflected both her attachment to Juanita and her incapacity to carry out the parenting role in a way that protects and nurtures the child."

In a careful review of this case at a conference attended also by two psychiatrists and a social worker, the child developmentalist stated: "My strong conviction is that Juanita must be moved into a home in which the damage to her social and emotional development can be repaired as much as possible. Ideally, she would be adopted by parents who are aware that it will take time and patience, along with love, for the healing of her spirit to occur and for her development to move forward."

Our guiding principles include the presumption that children should be maintained in their own homes whenever possible. On the basis of this presumption, the worker vigorously attempted to create and support a more adequate environment for Juanita so that she could grow up in the care of her biological mother. When this plan failed and after prolonged deliberation and several evaluations, the worker reluctantly took the step of removing the child from the home. The clinical assessment of the child revealed severe impairment of her cognitive and social development. The presumption that Juanita should be kept at home thus was overcome.

Soon before Juanita's third birthday, CPS obtained custody of her and placed her with a foster family, who seemed ideally suited to her particular needs. They were aware of "how bright and special she is and cared about her in a very loving and generous way." Although this was a temporary placement, the family made an immediate and strong attachment to Juanita despite their uncertainty about the duration of her stay.

When Juanita was 38 months old, after clinical consultation CPS filed a petition for termination of parental rights, which Mrs. Hogan contested. As part of the pending litigation, the court ordered another evaluation. A child psychiatrist and a senior social worker conducted three interviews with Mrs. Hogan. During one of these, she was observed in interaction with Juanita, whom she had been visiting regularly. The child's developmental progress was assessed both in this context and in an individual session with her foster mother. Juanita appeared to relate more warmly to the latter. The child psychiatrist now found Juanita's motor performance to be only slightly below age level; her language performance was about six months delayed. The results, therefore, suggested a degree of improvement that was attributable to her new environment. The tragic history of Mrs. Hogan need not be reviewed here. Her mental illness was well documented and evidenced itself not only in her general life-style but also in flamboyantly psychotic ideas and paranoid delusions.

The decision to remove Juanita from her mother's care, as made by CPS and buttressed by the consulting experts, was not based on the mother's schizophrenia. It should be emphasized that the presence of mental illness per se should not and does not disqualify any individual from parenting a child. Children raised by psychotic parents may indeed develop normally. In fact, the CPS staff hoped that the many services made available to Mrs. Hogan would enable her to provide adequate care for her daughter at home.

Unfortunately, two factors worked against the fulfillment of these expectations. First, Mrs. Hogan was unable to acknowledge her illness or to accept treatment that might ameliorate it. She could not view realistically either her condition or its effect on Juanita. Second, her unpredictable behavior prevented her from providing an even minimally adequate environment for her daughter. She was incapable of offering Juanita stimulation or of mediating her contact with the outside world. In this case, the mother's thought disturbance increasingly jeopardized the child's development and emotional well-being. The situation was the more tragic because Mrs. Hogan genuinely loved the child in the only way she could.

Juanita was placed with an adoptive family in another state soon after her fourth birthday. She made an excellent adjustment to this family and soon was talking spontaneously. Her development resumed a progressive course.

Regrettably, when the adoptive mother-to-be became pregnant, she and her husband decided that they did not wish to go forward with the adoption. After seven months in this home and with a minimum of preparation, Juanita was returned to the custody of the state. She was then placed with a foster mother who reported concern about Juanita's temper tantrums and her difficulty relating to other children at school. Juanita never disclosed to this foster mother or to her CPS worker anything about her stay with or traumatic rejection by the adoptive family.

An examination by the clinical expert who had previously evaluated Juanita revealed her to be depressed and slipping further behind in her development. This expert recommended, as did the CPS worker, that while awaiting another adoptive family Juanita be admitted to a small inpatient psychiatric service for children. This therapeutic milieu enabled the increasingly vulnerable child to work through some of her feelings about the painful disruptions in her life.

Considerations in this case:

1. For more than three years, the worker—who was empathic to both the mother and the child—observed the widening gap between the mother's ability to nurture the child and the child's needs. Multiple support services failed to compensate for the mother's disability. Developmental and psychological testing as well as conferences with a variety of professionals were used to

monitor Juanita's progress and needs so that every alternative could be explored before removing the child from her home.

2. As discussed above, neglect and deprivation were observed to be causing emotional and cognitive damage to the child and, at times, were associated with a lack of physical safety.

3. Although in a sense this case can be seen as an exception to our developmental principles, in that abuse and neglect as usually interpreted were absent, in another respect it exemplifies the assumption that "every child needs and deserves to feel secure in his or her home environment. Security involves both the physical and emotional well-being of the child."* After prolonged deliberation, this child was removed from the home because the alternative course had been documented as dangerous. A detailed assessment of parent and child revealed that the presumption against removal had been overcome and that the principle of the least detrimental alternative had been adhered to. Tragically, the delay in achieving permanency for this child was associated with great damage.

Follow-up:
The original foster family, having felt deeply the loss of this child, now applied to become her adoptive parents. They gradually became involved with Juanita and the treatment plan while the child was in the hospital.

CASE 7
Peter. Newborn child of mentally ill parents; co-terminous petition filed.

In some instances it is imperative that termination of parental rights be considered at the time of an infant's birth. This was the case with Peter Johnson, who at birth was seen to be at imminent risk. The personalities and actions of his parents were such as to threaten serious physical damage to him and perhaps to endanger his life.

*See appendix 1.

A hospital psychiatrist examined Peter's 26-year-old mother on three successive days because of her "floridly psychotic behavior" immediately before and after the baby's birth. The diagnosis of schizophrenia was based not only on this assessment but also on her previous history. This included multiple psychiatric hospitalizations and an inability to comply with outpatient psychiatric treatment. Her three other children had been removed from her care and subsequently adopted. The psychiatrist observed that Mrs. Johnson was unable to interact appropriately with the new infant. He noted that "she deteriorates into hysterical outbursts" in response to the infant's cries and demands. She was unable to recognize his needs, for example, when he was choking. The psychiatrist determined that Mrs. Johnson was mentally incompetent, and she was discharged to a psychiatric hospital for continued treatment the following week.

Peter's 22-year-old father was observed by hospital physicians to be "overtly psychotic, volatile, and grossly inappropriate." Because his general behavior and acknowledgment of homicidal ideas aroused concern for the safety of the baby and medical personnel (whom he had threatened), Mr. Johnson was restricted from visiting. In a letter to CPS the hospital psychiatrist stated that the infant was at risk of lethal injury if released to the care of either parent. Peter was placed in foster care directly from the hospital. CPS subsequently filed a co-terminous petition, which the parents contested. The court then requested an evaluation of Peter and his parents, to address the question of whether the parents had the capacity to care for him. Peter's parents were interviewed by a psychiatrist, and a pediatrician/child development expert examined the 4-month-old baby. The professionals' report follows in part:

> Peter is developing adequately for his age . . . but is not a robust baby. He seems to be a more than ordinarily sensitive child who needs skillful child care adapted to his sen-

sitivities. . . . Without these conditions his development would be placed at risk. . . .

Peter's parents have led a very marginal existence. . . . Mr. Johnson was markedly guarded and suspicious, with speech occasionally disorganized. He seemed unable to comprehend the difficulties and complexities entailed in the process of infant care. He exhibited poor judgment and lack of insight. He described a very restricted existence in which he functions as Mrs. Johnson's primary caretaker . . . regarding her need to take medication. Mrs. Johnson is a markedly disheveled and disorganized woman. She did not appear capable of meeting the needs of an infant or of a young child. She expected that the baby would sleep through the night because he was a "good" baby.

When Peter was 2½ years old, CPS again requested an evaluation to assess his progress and needs, both to guide his foster mother in caring for him and to consider the desirability of visitation by his biological mother. The follow-up indicated the child's continuing psychological vulnerability. The clinical experts strongly advised against visitation by Peter's chronically ill biological mother.

Considerations in this case:

1. This case illustrates the need for rapid, careful planning for an infant in jeopardy. The younger the child, the more urgent is the need for the swift development of a plan.

2. CPS worked effectively with hospital physicians in developing such a plan.

3. Expert assessment was sought to confirm or refute the presumption that termination was in the child's best interests.

4. The clinical experts observed that the mother was actively psychotic. As mentioned before, a parent's mental illness is not in itself a sufficient basis on which to sever the parent-child relationship. In this case, assessment revealed that the parents' behavior

and their unwillingness to accept services supported the plan for termination. This was a controversial recommendation. Because the child had never been in the parents' care, there was no evidence that his physical safety would be jeopardized. The parents had been considered too impaired to care for their child.

Follow-up:
When Peter was about 3 years old, parental rights were terminated and he was adopted by his foster mother.

CASE 8
Alfred. Newborn child with inadequate mother, leading to an Order of Temporary Custody.

The situation of Alfred Valli also demanded immediate planning. This baby was referred at birth to CPS by the hospital's social services department. His mother, aged 21, was well known to various community agencies. Ms. Valli's early life had been marked by neglect. By the time she was 18 months old, she was in the custody of the welfare commissioner, her mother having been hospitalized for a mental illness. Ms. Valli was placed in four foster homes during the years that followed; in one of them, she was severely mistreated—for example, locked in closets and often left alone.

Ms. Valli had had difficulties at school and required special educational services. As a child, teenager, and young adult, she had been evaluated at several mental health clinics, where her emotional neediness and intellectual limitations were repeatedly diagnosed. None of the various treatment programs in which she had been involved—speech therapy, adolescent group therapy, vocational counseling, individual therapy, and two psychiatric hospitalizations—had been able to help her. An educational and training program also failed, and she left the services of a state rehabilitation center after a few months.

When Alfred was born, the hospital staff viewed his mother as incapable of caring for him. The alleged father denied paternity.

One year earlier Ms. Valli had been described by a mental health clinic psychiatrist as "childlike . . . and barely able to function on her own." The hospital report referred to her "limitations and emotional deprivation." When Alfred was 4 days old, Ms. Valli took him from the hospital. That evening she was found sitting with the baby on a doorstep in the rain. A cousin took them in for the night. Ms. Valli did not attempt to care for the baby but asked her cousin to feed him, saying that she "didn't feel like it."

When Alfred was 6 days old, CPS obtained an Order of Temporary Custody and placed the baby in a foster home. During this time, CPS referred Ms. Valli for rehabilitative treatment both to help her develop a capacity for parenting and to control her violent temper. When the baby was 5 months old, Ms. Valli married a man twenty years her senior, in part because she believed that if she was married the baby would be returned to her. Her husband's history included chronic health problems, two psychiatric hospitalizations, and the inability to care for his own three children.

When Alfred was 7 months old, an effort was made to reunite him with his mother. The reunion, however, was short-lived. After four days, the baby had failed to settle in, had lost weight, and was increasingly disorganized in his behavior. When his mother sought medical care, he was readmitted to the hospital with the diagnosis of nonorganic failure to thrive. An irritable, colicky baby, he was noted to have very poor sleep and eating patterns and delayed vocal responses. Again CPS obtained an Order of Temporary Custody, and three weeks later Alfred was returned to his foster family, who had visited him daily in the hospital. At this time, despite a special diet, Alfred's height, weight, and head size had dropped below the lowest percentile curve.

Alfred underwent several assessments between birth and 14 months of age. He continued to be a silent baby whose vocabulary was limited to the few words he had acquired as a 1-year-old. His foster mother was distressed by the child's extreme motor activity, which coincided with his beginning to walk. He habitually rushed about the house, destroyed toys, and banged his head when frustrated, once making a dent in the wall. Referred for neurological and developmental assessment at age 2½, Alfred was described as "hyperactive, developmentally delayed with microcephaly. . . . The etiology of his disturbed personality is undoubtedly a complicated interaction of constitutional vulnerability and reactions to distressing experiences such as . . . gastrointestinal problems and the sudden separation from his foster mother, followed by extreme neglect for a few days with the resulting 3 week hospitalization. . . . A very disturbed little boy whose future learning and personality development are very much at risk."

When Alfred was 31 months old, his foster mother indicated her wish to adopt him. Consequently, CPS filed a termination petition, which was contested by Ms. Valli. A court order required another evaluation of Alfred and his mother to assess the latter's parenting abilities, the likelihood that she could be rehabilitated, and the nature of her relationship with her son.

As part of this process, a child psychiatrist from a mental health clinic saw Alfred for developmental assessments on several occasions: alone, in interaction with his biological mother, and in the presence of his foster mother. The same psychiatrist also interviewed the foster mother separately and, together with a social worker/consultant, met on two occasions with the biological mother for evaluative purposes. Alfred was evaluated also by a psychologist whose specialty was speech and communications disorders. Prior to this extensive reevaluation, the decision of CPS to press for termination of parental rights had been based on the belief that Alfred was in jeopardy, since his mother appeared to be an incompetent caretaker who had failed in several efforts at rehabilitation. She appeared to have no significant relationship with the child and no capacity to form one. The evaluations by professionals in child development and psychiatry supported the CPS actions. As their assessments and recommendations stated,

Alfred is clearly at risk for continued difficulties and his subsequent development and prognosis will depend on the adequacy of his caretaking experience. . . . He needs a stable and consistent environment and would be a challenge even to an experienced mother. . . . Given the long history of his relationship with his foster mother, it is not surprising that he relates to her as his psychological parent. He has essentially no psychological relationship with Ms. Valli. . . . Alfred's foster mother is well aware of his needs. She clearly is attached to him and he to her. She would be willing to participate in a subsidized adoption and indicated her willingness to allow Ms. Valli continued visitation. The foster mother clearly functions as Alfred's mother and disrupting this relationship would compound his difficulties and add to this tragic situation. Accordingly, termination of parental rights is recommended.

Considerations in this case:

1. The removal of a child from his biological mother at birth necessitated the formulation of both immediate and long-range plans.

2. Since the mother was disorganized and had experienced chronic difficulties in adaptation to life (attributed by some workers in part to her own early deprivation and disrupted care), there was concern about her competence to care for her newborn child.

3. A treatment plan was developed that was designed to compensate for the mother's inadequacies and provide the baby with a constant and affectionate primary caretaker. The plan included provision of rehabilitative services, based on the mother's manifest desire and willingness to care for the child. It failed.

4. An additional issue here is that a baby who had spent almost the entire seven months of his life with a foster mother was subjected to the trial of being returned to his biological mother. Regardless of the mother's needs, the baby's best interests would have been better served had he stayed continuously in the care of his

foster mother, the only home he had ever known. Experimentation should not be undertaken in the service of a legal strategy.

Follow-up:

When he was 4 years and 6 months old, Alfred was reevaluated by the child psychiatrist who had previously assessed him. His biological mother had relinquished her parental rights, and Alfred had continued to live with his original foster family. The psychiatrist found that Alfred had made "impressive" progress, "a testament to the quality of care he has received," as well as to a special-education program. The degree of improvement in his language skills was especially noteworthy. It was hoped that his foster family would proceed with plans for a subsidized adoption.* A year later they did. (It is most unfortunate that because of state requirements the completion of the adoption procedure takes so long.)

CASE 9

Iris, Dorinda, and Andy. Long-term neglect; abuse difficult to substantiate.

The Ungar case provides another illustration of planned removal from the home, but presents a less clear-cut situation than the previous cases.

Mrs. Ungar, married at 16 and imprisoned three times for shoplifting, by the age of 33 had given birth to five children by four different men. (The two oldest sons, victims of severe abuse and neglect and already in the custody of CPS, were not included in the evaluation discussed below.) This family's history was complicated further by the presence of osteogenesis imperfecta, a bone disease that afflicted Mrs. Ungar, her daughter Dorinda, and Andy, her youngest child. Iris, the older daughter, suffered a congenital condition of a different sort, a bilateral rotation of the tibia,

---

*This subsidy is an acknowledgment that continuity with the same foster family should include extra financial provisions for the care of children with special needs.

which required braces and active medical monitoring. Because of these congenital problems, the causes of the children's frequent injuries were, at times, difficult for medical examiners to determine. In addition, Mrs. Ungar repeatedly failed to bring the children to their appointments for necessary medical care.

Iris frequently had bruises, mostly on her face and neck. Later it was learned that she had also been punished by cold baths. On several occasions she was evaluated as developmentally delayed. Dorinda and Andy endured various injuries, including dog bites. They were hospitalized on separate occasions for multiple bruises and for failure to thrive.

Over the years, CPS facilitated and coordinated the services of numerous social agencies to assist Mrs. Ungar. These included the parent enrichment program of a child guidance center and various hospital clinics (pediatric, orthopedic, neurological, learning and developmental disabilities). Mrs. Ungar and her children did not benefit from these services. The children's deterioration dramatized the failure of all efforts to assist them. In successive years, the three children were placed in foster care for two periods of one month each at their mother's request.

Despite the energetic efforts of the CPS social worker to find one foster placement for the three children, she was ultimately forced to settle for three separate foster homes for Iris, age 5, Dorinda, 3, and Andy, who was 1 year old. On the grounds of severe neglect, which included physical endangerment of the children, the worker took action and pressed forward with a coterminous petition. This petition was buttressed by the report of a child psychiatrist, prepared for the court, which included interviews with the children and several with Mrs. Ungar, as well as psychological testing. In summary, the clinical expert indicated that these children had suffered from repeated physical insults and dangerous lack of care, which put them at imminent risk of serious harm, and that their mother was unable to protect and nurture them.

Considerations in this case:

1. The decision to remove the children and to seek termination of their mother's parental rights was based on the documented deterioration in the children's level of functioning—a result of severe neglect, including physical endangerment. In such families, repeated follow-up assessments are of great importance in order to track the course of the children's development and to indicate appropriate revision of services and placement plans.

2. The mother's repeated failure to use appropriate recommended services to assist the family reinforced this decision.

3. Severe medical neglect, in view of the children's special needs, played a particularly important role. The presence of osteogenesis imperfecta complicated and obscured the question of abuse.

4. The presence of osteogenesis imperfecta, a chronic and life-threatening disease, would prove a challenge to any family. Support services can help parents provide their children, if so afflicted, with adequate care.

5. Our foster-care resources often make it difficult—at times impossible—to place all siblings with one foster family. This effort to place siblings together is based on the continuity principle, to enable siblings to maintain their community of interests and their common experiences (see pp. 138–142 for discussion of siblings).

Follow-up:
See Case 25.

CASE 10
Flora. Child removed from home at 3 months after services failed, with many ensuing placements.

When children have established primary or very strong relationships with surrogate parents, have lost their primary relationships to their biological parents or never developed such relationships, and when the surrogate parents are prepared to keep them permanently and a clinical judgment is made that the children's long-range development will be threatened by their removal from the surrogate parents, all efforts should be made within the law to enable those children to remain with the surrogate parents.*

Flora Young was referred to CPS at birth as being at risk. Flora's 27-year-old mother, a limited and emotionally needy person who herself had been abused as a child, was known to have had problems with drugs and alcohol. Five years earlier, she had voluntarily terminated her parental rights to her then 2-year-old son, who suffered extreme emotional deprivation and physical abuse while in her care. This child subsequently was adopted. Mrs. Young said she wanted to keep her second child and to do better by her.

With many weekly hours of support from a parent aide and a supervising social worker, all went reasonably well for three months—until the baby was brought to the emergency room with severe multiple facial bruises. Flora's father later admitted that, while under the influence of alcohol, he had injured the baby. Mrs. Young was unwilling to leave him.

From this point on, Flora had a series of caretakers. Under an Order of Temporary Custody, she spent six weeks with one foster family, two weeks with another foster mother, and then several weeks again with the original foster family; at 9 months, she was returned to her biological mother. Services were provided to help Mrs. Young with her parenting abilities as part of this reunification plan. They failed. For the third and last time, Flora was placed with her original foster parents until, one month later, they moved out of the state.

Consequently, at the age of 1 year, Flora went to yet another foster family, a move that represented her seventh change of home. Her adjustment there was described as "most adequate." The pre-

*See appendix 1.

vious foster parents also had found her a pleasant and easy baby to care for; healthy and alert, she had settled in well with each placement. At this time Mr. Young had already signed a voluntary consent to termination of parental rights. CPS filed a petition for termination of Mrs. Young's parental rights.

When Flora was almost 20 months old, a CPS team met several times to discuss the best placement for her. Two possibilities were considered, about which there was some difference of opinion: (1) that Flora remain with her present foster family, by whom she would be adopted, and (2) that she join her half-brother—with whom she had had little contact—whose adoptive mother, Mrs. Edmonds, had expressed a willingness to adopt Flora as well. Flora's caseworker favored the second plan. Among other factors influencing the worker was her belief that Mrs. Edmonds was a person of superior qualities who perhaps could, in the long run, provide Flora with a more satisfactory home than that of her present foster parents.

Those opposed to this plan took into account that Flora, settled in and doing well in her present home, had a history of many moves: four sets of caretakers and seven moves in twenty months. They emphasized her vulnerability and warned that moving her again might be highly traumatic.

The final CPS decision was that Flora should remain in her current home. After eight months, she had established a trusting relationship with these parents, who enjoyed her and who expressed the wish to care for her on a permanent basis, agreeing to cooperate with any programs deemed best for her. Arrangements were made for Flora and her half-brother to visit with each other regularly.

The resolution of this case was significant because it was determined primarily by the needs of the child. Moving her to the home of yet another stranger and away from people with whom she had begun to form a loving attachment could have jeopardized her development, which was progressing well.

Considerations in this case:

1. An abused 20-month-old child in her seventh placement was thriving after more than seven months with her current foster parents, who wished to adopt her.

2. Another potential caretaker offered the advantages of reuniting the child with her biological half-brother as well as greater material comforts and intellectual stimulation. This individual met the caseworker's notion of the better parent.

3. The worker had not sufficiently taken into account the attachment of the child to her present caretakers, with whom she had lived for almost eight of her twenty months, and the child's good progress in their care. These facts argued against the removal of the child. From a developmental viewpoint, at 20 months she could have been severely affected by the loss once again of a loving relationship.

Children Who Are Returned Home

Once the decision has been made to remove a child from his or her home, if there is any possibility of the child returning home, CPS and the parent(s) must immediately develop a plan for short- and long-term goals. It must be clearly explained to the parent(s) what changes need to be made, and how these changes can be implemented, before the child can be returned. A worker planning for the return of a child, therefore, should consider the reasons for the removal, changes in the family situation that would assure a safe and nurturing environment, and a plan to safeguard the child's attachments to significant parent and sibling figures. Frequent contact between parent(s) and child is essential.

Both the biological and the foster parents should be involved in preparing the child to return home. The age and developmental needs of the child also should be taken into account. The younger the child, the more urgent is the need for the swift development of a permanent plan. Young children do not have the emotional and cognitive capacities to tolerate prolonged uncertainty and loss.

In cases involving infants in which CPS attempts a reunification, a plan must be made that assures the foster parents' willingness to cooperate and their reasonable proximity to the home of the biological mother so that she can visit with her baby for several hours three or four times a week, as well as participate in such services as agreed upon. If reunification is not the goal, CPS must vigorously pursue the termination of parental rights and a sound permanent placement, adoption usually being the most promising.

CASE 11

Harry, Mona, and Quigg. When is it safe to return children? (See Case 4.)

The Belsky case, one aspect of which was discussed in another section, illustrates a well-coordinated plan. After the emergency removal of a severely abused child and the mother's incarceration, her three other children were gradually returned to her.

Following a community team meeting, attended by a psychiatrist, a psychologist, a pediatrician, a probation officer, the director of a social agency, and the CPS worker, the case was referred for evaluation to a consultant social worker in an outside agency. During the team meeting, all but the CPS worker expressed opposition to the possibility of returning the children to their mother.

Because of the unknown nature of the mother's disturbance and the strong disagreement within the team about the mother's capacity to provide safety for her children, the consultant requested both psychiatric and psychological evaluations of Mrs. Belsky and a developmental examination of Mona.* In addition to these detailed and expert opinions, the consultant himself conducted five clinical interviews with Mrs. Belsky.

The consultant's report included previously unknown, but indispensable, background information. Mrs. Belsky, who felt re-

*The other children were developing satisfactorily.

jected by her mother and neglected by an alcoholic father, suffered
from pathologically low self-esteem. She had become involved
with hard drugs and sadistic boyfriends in adolescence and at age
18 or 19 married a drug dealer after becoming pregnant by him.
She was immensely relieved when this first child, Harry, was born
healthy, showing no signs of heroin or methadone addiction. She
enjoyed caring for him and believed that she had been "spared"
punishment. As described in Case 4, the congenital afflictions of
her second child confirmed Mrs. Belsky's worst fears, and Sophia
became the victim of her mother's perception of herself as "bad."
In the next two years both Mona and Quigg were born in good
health. Mona was especially cherished by her mother, who cared
for her with great tenderness. There was never any indication that
this mother had been abusive to any child except for Sophia. On
the contrary, those who visited her early on (a CPS worker and a
parent aide) were impressed by the apparent orderliness of her parenting and housekeeping efforts. During her ten months in prison,
Mrs. Belsky, aided by the CPS worker, kept in touch with Harry,
age 7, Mona, 3, and Quigg, 2. They visited her in prison at least
monthly, sometimes every two weeks, and they often spoke on the
telephone.

The clinical examinations revealed that Mrs. Belsky had a
strong desire to improve her life and suffered from an underlying
reactive depression. There was no evidence of psychotic thinking.
Despite questions raised by the experts, the consultant recommended that the children be returned to their mother's care. She
believed this plan to be a less detrimental alternative than their
remaining in the foster-care system.

Before plans were made for the children's return home, the stability and caretaking capacities of the mother were carefully assessed and important changes in her environment were noted. The
injured child, for whom parental rights had been terminated, had
been placed in an adoptive home. Upon her release on parole, Mrs.
Belsky entered a counseling program, found an apartment and a

job, and remained free of drugs and alcohol for close to a year.* She apparently had gained insight into her destructive behavior and was thought to have potential for further growth. The children likewise had been followed closely by CPS, and plans for their gradual return home, as recommended by the consultant, were under way.

Following the plan formulated during the evaluation, Harry, then 8, who had a strong tie to his mother, soon was returned to her and was seen to be developing well. Bolstered by the examiner's evaluation of Mona and aware of her strong wish to be with her mother and brother, the consultant recommended that the child be returned home as soon as her mother felt ready to take her. Mona and Quigg were already under their mother's care on weekend visits, with supervision by their grandmother. It was also recommended that 3-year-old Quigg gradually move from his foster home to his mother's. This transition was facilitated by the cooperative relationship that Mrs. Belsky had formed with the foster parent. In her recommendation, the consultant recognized that the plan was not without risks and that any return by the mother to substance abuse or assaultive partners would be cause for alarm.

Considerations in this case:

1. This case illustrates the use of consultation by a CPS worker. The aim was to determine the mother's capacity—after incarceration for the abuse of one child—to provide a safe home for her other three children. Seeking help for this difficult question, the worker consulted with an expert outside the agency. The consultant organized an assessment of the mother and a developmental evaluation of Mona.

2. In organizing team meetings the CPS worker and consultant enabled family members to use coordinated services rather than

*This was a condition of her probation and was documented by laboratory screening.

to seek each service separately. An ad hoc community group may find itself unable to be objective, especially in determining the least detrimental placement for certain children. There is a tendency in such a group for each member to declare his or her opposition to child abuse. As a result, ad hoc groups often seek to avoid risks rather than take those risks that are compatible with sound clinical judgment.

3. The consultant's assessment enabled the agency to assume the risks inevitably inherent in such a decision. The short-term predictions were cautiously favorable. Long-term predictions were not applied in the treatment planning because experience has demonstrated them to be unreliable. The agency gradually developed the clinical judgment that returning the children to their mother's care would be in their best interests. That is, it was the least detrimental alternative for the children.

4. To reduce the risks in the plan, the children's gradual return home was made contingent on certain conditions: protective supervision through regular visits by the CPS worker, counseling in a narcotics program and drug monitoring for the mother, and school reports to CPS about the children's progress. Psychotherapy for the mother was viewed as an important voluntary option.

5. The placement of the abused child in an adoptive home clearly served the best interests of that child and was the least detrimental alternative for her. The continuing reactions of her siblings and of her mother to her injury and to her removal from the home were unknown. The remaining children would, of course, worry about their absent sister, feel a deep sense of loss, and wonder to what extent her fate might become theirs.

The mother gradually developed insight into why she had damaged this child and why the child should not be raised by her. Aware of the anxiety of the siblings who were returned to her, however, the mother was confident that she could care for them in a safe and nurturing way.

Follow-up:

The follow-up one year later revealed that the plan was effective. Mrs. Belsky received support from her continuing contact with the foster mother. She also established a positive relationship with her own mother, who, to her surprise, was able to help with the children. The children continued to develop well. It was too soon to feel confident about the long-term future.

CASE 12

Karl. Presumption of co-terminous petition overcome on the basis of child psychiatrist's recommendation that child be returned home.

The case of Karl Wood presented the CPS staff with a peculiarly difficult problem. This 3-year and 9-month-old child was seen by his pediatrician on two successive days for swelling and tenderness of the scalp. The third day, because of a marked increase in these symptoms, he was hospitalized with the diagnosis of subgaleal hematosis (hemorrhage into the scalp). The blood loss necessitated a transfusion in the intensive care unit. In the absence of any fracture or external evidence of bruising, and even though there was no loss of hair on the scalp, the medical staff concluded that the injury could have resulted only from "violent" hair pulling.

The parents could not provide an explanation. Although they had a long history of marital difficulties, Mrs. Wood firmly denied that either she or her husband had injured Karl. She suggested repeatedly that the severe edema must have resulted from an undiagnosed medical problem.

Because of the severity of the injuries, CPS filed a co-terminous petition, which was contested by the parents. On obtaining an Order of Temporary Custody, CPS placed the child with his maternal grandparents.* Subsequently, the court requested an eval-

---

*A new law currently requires a more thorough home-study evaluation for a placement with relatives than was the practice at the time of this child's injury.

uation to assist it in its decision as to what would be the best permanent living arrangements for Karl. His mother had been charged formally with causing the injury.

A child psychiatrist interviewed Mrs. Wood three times, held a play interview with Karl, and conducted a developmental assessment of him. The psychiatrist also observed the mother-child relationship. The following information guided him in his recommendations: developmentally, Karl Wood was found to be functioning above his age level, especially in the areas of language and problem-solving skills. He seemed to be struggling to understand the reason for his separation from his mother, toward whom he appeared in no way fearful but, rather, loving and trusting. Mrs. Wood, a somewhat shy, withdrawn woman who had been in counseling for some time, discussed her concern for Karl—with whom she visited frequently—as well as her anger and frustration at her son's removal and the subsequent charges filed against her. Mrs. Wood's parents, brother, and sister-in-law likewise indicated most strongly that they could not believe that Mr. or Mrs. Wood had injured the child and voiced their anger at both the legal system and CPS for what they perceived as an unfair intrusion into their family life.

The psychiatrist's report included the following recommendations:

> . . . it should be noted that the injury remains unexplained and is likely to remain so. It is not exactly clear when or how it occurred [but] this evaluation must focus on the best interest of the child and the clinical material presented in this case. At the present time Karl Wood's best interest would appear to be served by returning him to his mother's care. This recommendation is not made lightly; the fact that the injury occurred and has not been explained continues to be a concern. However, Karl clearly has developed well in his mother's care, has suffered from the effects of his separation

from his mother and his siblings, and does not appear to have been either neglected or chronically exposed to an abusive situation. He and his mother are closely attached to each other and to separate them would put his development at some risk. Appropriate supervision and monitoring should be mandated for some period of time if Karl is, in fact, returned.

The psychiatrist's recommendation that Karl be returned to his mother's care provoked a strong reaction among community and CPS workers. The plan for a co-terminous petition was based on the life-threatening nature of the child's injury. The opinion expressed by the psychiatrist was an exception to the principle that children who have suffered such an injury should be permanently separated from the adult perpetrators.

Following the psychiatrist's evaluation, several concerned CPS staff members initiated a child protection meeting a week before the scheduled Juvenile Court hearing. This meeting, attended by some twenty individuals, was sponsored by a regional pediatrics department and included several senior consultants from this and other agencies, as well as professionals previously involved in the case.

The discussion focused in part on the uneasiness of CPS workers about the child's safety should he be returned home. The situation at home was unchanged; no perpetrator had been identified. Had the mother acknowledged her guilt (if indeed it existed) and her need to seek help, the situation would have been a more familiar one. Instead, it was feared that the family's hostility to CPS might interfere with the worker's ability to supervise Mrs. Wood or help in any way. The Family Service Association worker, Mrs. Wood's longtime counselor, dispelled these fears by consenting to provide the supervision and monitoring recommended by the court-designated child psychiatrist. Furthermore, the counselor believed that Mrs. Wood was innocent. She would not have agreed that the child should be returned home simply to assuage the mother. She was clinically convinced that the child would be safe and better off at home.

After this discussion, an entirely new medical interpretation was introduced by a senior physician from the regional department. In rare cases of subgaleal hematosis, a minor injury such as a slight bruise in a vulnerable area of the scalp can produce an oozing leak in the blood vessels that cumulatively could lead to the clinical condition that Karl developed. This expert believed that such an incident might well have occurred in this case. Furthermore, this diagnosis was substantiated by the absence of neurological damage.

Given the above evidence, along with the knowledge of the child's good development—he had been well nurtured and protected—the meeting concluded with an endorsement of the child psychiatrist's earlier recommendation. A senior child psychiatrist and pediatrician stated: "If Karl is returned to the mother, since how the injury happened is still unknown, it might happen again. But if the child is not returned to the mother, one can be sure that the team will be doing damage by breaking the mother-child relationship."

Considerations in this case:

1. The result of the child psychiatrist's evaluation was unexpected. Rather than support a co-terminous petition, his clinical judgment led him to believe that the child's best interests would be served by a reunification with his mother. This was the least detrimental alternative.

2. The CPS worker and the supervisor convened another team meeting to develop a case management plan. As the Guidelines state, "It is expected that the public and private sectors will work together to ensure the provision of the full spectrum of voluntary

services needed to provide meaningful support to children and families."* Such collaboration is crucial in cases where there is disagreement or lack of clarity.

3. The expert medical consultation was of particular importance because it provided an alternative explanation for the injury. Had the injury been taken only at face value, this mother most likely would have been further misjudged. Instead, the new presumptive diagnosis supported the controversial recommendation of the child psychiatrist.

4. The team consensus was that this was a puzzling, complicated case, described several times as "unsettling." Despite precautions, there is often a heightened anxiety about returning a child home when there is no clear explanation for his or her injury.

5. When there is no convincing explanation of how the injury occurred, it is useful to accept the limits of our knowledge in determining the least detrimental alternative.

Follow-up:

Three years later, Mrs. Wood wrote a letter to the child guidance clinic where her son had been evaluated. She summarized her reaction as follows:

> Three years ago, my son was taken from me because of a false allegation.
>
> Thanks to the doctor on your staff, my son was returned home.
>
> Today, I hope no one else goes through what my son and my family suffered because of a false allegation.
>
> Thank you again.

This letter is a useful reminder of the harm that sometimes results from even the most carefully considered clinical judgments.

*See appendix 1.

Children Who Remain at Home or Are Returned Home with Services

The policy of CPS is to maintain children in their own homes whenever possible. The provision of adequate support services to counteract deficiencies in the home is often the least detrimental alternative. Such decisions must, of course, be based on specific assessments of both parents and child and must take into account such factors as physical danger to the child and failure to meet his or her vital needs. Recent models of family preservation services indicate that maintaining the child in the home with support services is an increasingly desirable option.

CASE 13

Felicity, Jared, and Hiram. Children who can remain home, with services.

Felicity, Jared, and Hiram Jenkins, 1, 4, and 8 years old, were referred to CPS following Felicity's hospitalization. Unobserved by her mother, the baby had inhaled cocaine and ingested unidentified pills. When she became lethargic, Ms. Jenkins and her mother, Mrs. Baxter, responded appropriately by seeking immediate medical care, and Felicity was hospitalized. The state filed criminal charges against Ms. Jenkins of risk of injury to a minor.

After careful observation, Felicity was released from the hospital to her mother's care. The decision to return the child to her mother was based partly on Ms. Jenkins's devoted presence during the hospitalization, as well as on an agreement with CPS that Ms. Jenkins enter into drug treatment, arrange for her children's safety, and cooperate with an in-home family support service agency. Mrs. Baxter agreed to assist and support her daughter in carrying out the plans described in the agreement.

Unfortunately, Ms. Jenkins was unable to live up to these commitments. Against medical advice, she left a hospital drug treatment program after forty-eight hours. Her mother was unable to dissuade her but continued to care for the children. Ms. Jenkins also was unable to sustain her contact and efforts to work with two other mental health centers as an outpatient. Four months after Felicity's hospitalization and the initial involvement of CPS, the court ordered Ms. Jenkins to enter a ninety-day drug treatment program.

During this time, the continuing efforts of the family support service agency were of crucial importance. A support service worker spent three to four hours daily several days a week in the children's home helping to care for them and being supportive of Mrs. Baxter. A clinician supervised the support worker and met once a week with Mrs. Baxter. As noted by the support service agency, Ms. Jenkins was a young mother who loved and wanted her children, but who was handicapped by her cocaine addiction, as well as by chronic underlying depression. Her interaction with her children, who reciprocated her affection for them, was "adequate but joyless." If Ms. Jenkins was unable to follow through with the recommended treatments, the agency suggested that CPS consider giving Mrs. Baxter custody of her grandchildren. The important presence of the other three grandparents strengthened the effort to keep the children at home as a family.

Ms. Jenkins successfully completed the ninety-day drug treatment program. Her physical and psychological outlook had improved significantly. In a visit with the family support worker, accompanied by Mrs. Baxter and Felicity, Ms. Jenkins reported her progress with pride and enthusiasm. She was eager to return to some form of clerical work, which she had enjoyed after high school before she first became pregnant. Mrs. Baxter told the support worker, "If it weren't for you and the family program, none of this would have happened." She added, "You helped me to help my daughter and grandchildren. Thank you."

Considerations in this case:

1. A family support service, despite many odds, enabled three children to remain in their home and family. During the court-

ordered absence of the mother for rehabilitation, the family support service buttressed the ability of the maternal grandmother to provide the children with continuing care.

2. Family integrity was maintained, and the children's development was protected and nurtured. Family support services indirectly enabled a young mother to resume her maternal role.

CASE 14

Paul. A child successfully returned home, with services.

Paul Calleia, age 2½ months, was left for the evening with a "friend of a friend" of his 18-year-old mother, Ms. Karloski. Paul, who had been unwell that day, later became severely dehydrated and was brought to a hospital emergency room by the acquaintance. His mother, who could not be found, was charged with neglect.

Upon discharge from the hospital, Paul was placed in foster care, committed to CPS, and was placed two more times before he was 7 months of age. After five months of placement, CPS referred Paul and his mother for in-home family support services in the hope that mother and son could thrive and be reunited.

Ms. Karloski came from a chaotic background, which included four full siblings, six half-siblings, an alcoholic father, and a physically abusive stepfather. She had never felt wanted by her mother and had lived apart from her family since the age of 13 in various settings, including foster care and group residence. Paul's father, who had a history of substance abuse and legal problems, abandoned Ms. Karloski before Paul's birth.

Ms. Karloski was initially described by the family service staff as emotionally immature, impulsive, and untrusting. However, she soon developed a trusting relationship with the parent aide and the clinician with whom she met four times per week. In the context of a therapeutic alliance, she became more responsive and gradually took control of her life. She was reinstated onto city welfare and began working in a Job Fair program. She visited with Paul frequently and regularly.

During this time, Ms. Karloski moved from unsuitable living arrangements and obtained a subsidized apartment. She followed through with such tasks as scheduling and keeping medical appointments for Paul and attending parenting classes. Daytime visits between mother and son progressed to unsupervised overnight stays, and at 10 months Paul was returned to his mother's care. The parent aide and the clinician gradually phased out their home visits and discontinued them altogether by Paul's first birthday.

At the time the case was closed, the agency noted:

> Ms. Karloski and Paul have developed a close bond. She has made exceptional strides in capably mothering him. She has received some support from her own family of origin. Ms. Karloski finds it difficult to acknowledge all that she has accomplished in a few months. She looks forward to continuing her own growth through her therapy with a psychiatric nurse and through participation in a group for new mothers. She has accomplished the responsibility of a full-time parent with a maturity that increases daily.

Considerations in this case:

1. Many services were activated that enabled this mother to resume her own development.

2. Through these sustained efforts, which led to the renewal of the mother-child relationship, the child's own healthy development was supported.

CASE 15

Marie and Walter. An example of false reporting.

Ms. Casey, a 30-year-old single working mother, was investigated by CPS upon the complaint of neighbors, who perceived her yelling at 4-year-old Marie and 2-year-old Walter at dinnertime as evidence of violence. The evaluation by CPS revealed no abuse or significant neglect, and they withdrew from and closed the case. Ms. Casey was bitter that there was no formal way in which the false allegation could be publicly withdrawn. She wished the "authorities" would reassure her neighbors that she was a devoted, competent mother who yelled at her children when their behavior and her state of fatigue led to her "blowing off steam." She wanted her worried neighbors to know "officially" that she was not an abusive, neglectful, abandoning parent, since she felt she had been "officially" investigated as such. Ms. Casey said wryly, "In my family, yelling is a way of making a point, not a sin, especially when you love and admire your children as I do and my family has done for three generations."

CASE 16

Nelson. A fatal outcome, despite many services.

This case ended in disaster, despite the best judgment and unusual efforts of a variety of professionals and agencies. Although each decision made or action taken appeared at the time to be the "right" one, the child died.

Nelson Parish was born to white middle-class parents in their mid-twenties who had been married for six years. He suffered a fractured arm at the age of 1 month. Twenty-four hours later, the parents sought medical aid. The mother explained that the baby had rolled off the couch and hit a glass table. No referral to CPS was made because the pediatrician believed the fracture to be the result of carelessness and did not consider these parents to be abusers. Nelson also was noted to have a small cataract.

Sixteen months later and two weeks after Nelson had undergone cataract surgery, he was hospitalized for multiple bruises and scratches, some of which were bizarre: scratches behind both ears, a bruise that encircled his right nipple, bruises and bite marks on his feet, toes, and one buttock. An X-ray revealed a healing fracture of one elbow. The parents were unable to explain the latter, but the mother acknowledged with embarrassment that over the past several months she had been giving her child "affectionate" bites.

The hospital referred the case to CPS. During a home visit,

the mother told the worker that she was having difficulty with Nelson's feedings. Although the pediatrician reassured her that skipping a few meals would not harm the child, the mother remained apprehensive. She did not acknowledge directly to the pediatrician or to the protective worker that she was struggling with her own aggressive impulses toward the child. Instead, she sought assistance for managing him. She asked for help with his temper tantrums, for example, which were especially troublesome to her because they resembled those she was said to have had at the same age. She also spoke of her fear that the baby would drown in his bath.

Over the next five months, many social service supports were provided to this family. Nelson initially was seen twice daily by a visiting nurse, who administered post-cataract-surgery eyedrops and continued daily visits when she recognized the mother's need for support. She considered Mrs. Parish to be isolated, lonely, and beset by feelings of inadequacy, but not abusive. A psychologist evaluated the parents and child and recommended other services, all of which the parents accepted: attendance at a child guidance clinic, an early stimulation program, and parenting classes. The psychologist assessed the parents as not abusive, an opinion shared by the pediatrician.

After several months the situation seemed to be improving, and the parents, together with CPS, agreed that the case could be closed at the end of the winter. In February the child had a swollen bruise on his forehead, but Mrs. Parish explained that he had lost his balance. Otherwise everything appeared to be going well; in fact, the family had taken a vacation together. In mid-March, the CPS worker made the last of twenty visits to the family. She noted affectionate exchanges between Nelson and his mother. Mrs. Parish reported that Nelson's temper tantrums were fewer and less severe. He also was eating better and continued to make good weight gain. Based on the worker's observations of the improved interaction between mother and child, she closed the case.

During this last visit, Mrs. Parish told the worker that although it had been hard for her to recognize her need for help, she was grateful for the agency's involvement. She enumerated the problems with which she had been struggling, including her limited understanding of child development, her problems in feeding her child, her difficulty developing confidence as a nurturing parent, and financial stress. She probably also was reacting unwittingly to Nelson's eye defect, which in retrospect may have been a significant (and overlooked) factor in her ambivalent and unsafe care of the baby. Thanks to the worker's assistance, Mrs. Parish said, there had been improvement in all these areas. Two weeks later, at the age of 22 months, Nelson was dead. He died of an acute traumatic subdural hematoma.

After this tragic ending, CPS initiated a discussion of the case in conjunction with clinical consultants, in part with the aim of analyzing and understanding the still-intense reactions of both workers and supervisors. Staff members reported their initial reaction as one of disbelief and shock, especially since the parents seemed to have followed the agreed-upon treatment plan. As staff members accepted the reality of the child's death, they experienced a marked increase in anxiety, depression, and a sense of helplessness. Workers were sad about the baby's death and felt guilty about and responsible for the event. They also feared possible legal prosecution, loss of employment, or both. They experienced a loss of self-esteem and a diminished sense of their professional competence. Workers reported feeling pain and anguish, along with the fear of having overlooked essential signals that might have averted the outcome.

In addition to these internal feelings of inadequacy and guilt, the workers expressed their anger. They were outraged by the parents, whose murderous aggression had been directed against the young child. They were angry at their supervisors and others within their own system for not being more effective in providing training, support, and resources adequate to avoid such a disaster, and they were angry with themselves for their human imperfections.

The workers' anger, fear, and guilt led to defensiveness and the need to blame others. These reactions interfered with the ability of the agency staff to support one another and to explore fully the case material to gain knowledge for application to future work.

Considerations in this case:

1. No single event more seriously strains child protection workers than the death or severe injury of a child in their care, especially when the child's parent is the aggressor.

2. No egregious errors were made on the part of the professionals, although in retrospect, as with any case, the material can be interpreted as revealing that insufficient attention was paid to the child's repeated injuries.

3. Workers and supervisors often understandably react defensively to so traumatic an event. This may impede their ability to manage their highly charged emotions, as well as their capacity to learn from these tragedies the lessons they can teach us for future children at risk.

4. In such cases, agencies must balance the need to respond quickly to public concern, as dramatized by the media, with the equally important need to enable staff members to cope with such tragedies and to maintain a high level of competence for future work with children and their parents.

5

Areas

of

Further

Concern

Sexual Abuse—Evaluation and Disposition

In sexual abuse cases the basis for decisions to remove children from their families is the same as that in cases of physical abuse, but with some special aspects. For example, the worker will need to distinguish between assault and seduction. Cases of sexual abuse, much like those of physical abuse, fall along a spectrum from extremely severe or life-threatening assaults, which carry the presumption that the child must be protected permanently from the abuser, to incestuous seductions, where counseling or psychotherapy or both may be the intervention of choice. In either case, assuming that one can establish a safe environment, it is best to maintain the child in her or his family if possible so that the psychological effects of separation do not further compound the trauma.

As Crewdson (1988) points out, "The psychological consequences of sexual abuse are far too little understood. What is known is that . . . not many children emerge from such an experience unscathed" (p. 207). Excessive stimulation—that is, excitement beyond a child's capacity to tolerate it—is overwhelming to the child. Whereas sexual exploration between individuals of the same age is not necessarily traumatic, sexual activities where significant age or developmental discrepancies exist can leave the child feeling overwhelmed, disorganized, confused, or frightened. The trauma of being exploited by an adult or by a person who is larger and more powerful is compounded when a parent is involved. Feelings of betrayal of trust by the very persons to whom the child looks for protection, nourishment, and consistency can result in irreconcilable distress, anger, and conflict. Feelings of excitement and pleasure may coexist with those of shame and guilt. The child also often feels permanently physically injured. Incapable of coping with or integrating such conflicting elements and overwhelming stimuli, the child may regress and become fixated, unable to function at the expected level of development.

Other reactions experienced by sexually abused children include a lowering of self-esteem and a distortion of body image. Although not specific to sexual abuse, manifest disturbances in behavior also may ensue. These include social withdrawal, excessive masturbation, promiscuity, and attempts to turn an experience of passive helplessness into activity through assault or seduction of other children and adults. Children who are abused sexually react in many different ways, depending on their age, level of development, and particular strengths and vulnerabilities. As Lewis and Sorrel (1968) point out, "No single sign is [indicative] of a disturbance resulting from sexual assault" (p. 797). Rather, specific symptoms are related more to the child's level of development and to the context in which the sexual assault took place.

In addition to the worker's assessment of the child's safety and a decision about placement, a single physical examination of the child by a familiar or experienced pediatrician is often indicated. This need is apparent in cases involving questions of venereal disease (gonorrhea, syphilis, genital herpes, and AIDS) and in cases where there is alleged trauma to the vagina or rectum, including perforated hymen with widened vaginal opening, or evidence of sperm in the vagina or rectum. In less obvious situations it is important to consult with a pediatrician to determine whether the child's physical status is normal and to assure the child of his or her physical integrity. It is neither helpful nor appropriate for others, such as workers, teachers, or the police, to take on the physician's role in examining the child physically.* Such an exami-

---

*Just as it would be inappropriate for a physician or nurse to assume the role of investigator, it is inappropriate for anyone other than a qualified health professional to carry out a gynecological examination on a child.

nation could constitute an unnecessary, traumatic intrusion for the child, leading to overstimulation, feelings of discomfort, injury, shame, or self-consciousness. Some workers who are accustomed to viewing bruises or other markings of physical abuse on a child's body have mistakenly assumed that pulling down a child's trousers to examine her or his genitals is a comparable procedure in cases of sexual abuse.

In addition to the referral to a pediatrician, the worker will want to expedite referral of the child and family to a mental health agency—not for purposes of "detective work" but to assess possible treatment needs. In her article "The Unmet Psychiatric Needs of Sexually Abused Youths," Christine Adams-Tucker (1984) states that "protective service colleagues should work with child psychiatrists in a salutary way in order to ensure that all sexually molested children are identified to the best of our combined abilities and that they obtain the necessary mental health care." She notes that often "the child's needs remain on the periphery and he or she risks being given no individual services at all" (p. 659).* The sexually abused child requires individual assessment to determine what his or her needs may be.

Even for those who are trained as child experts, without medical corroboration it may be impossible ever to know what a child has experienced. Whether or not the alleged abuse can be documented or ascertained, the child expert plays an important role. The expert assesses and describes the child's developmental status and the quality of her or his relationship to important adults, as

---

*Workers might be interested in Dr. Adams-Tucker's findings that "several biases may be operating in referral for psychiatric care of officially reported sexually abused children. The likelihood of reaching the guidance clinic by referral from the child protection agency is *diminished* for a child who is a black boy, older than 10 years of age when first sexually abused, and residing in a mother-headed household. Biases which are operating which increase the likelihood of referral to the child guidance clinic favor those who are white girls, younger than 10 years of age when first molested, and who live in a two-parent family" (p. 665).

well as the adults' capacity to protect and adequately nurture the child's growth. The purpose of such an assessment ultimately is to decide whether to recommend treatment or other appropriate services.

It is recommended that "anatomically correct" dolls be used only by child experts. There are at present no reliable data to suggest that play with such dolls can be interpreted as an accurate historical rendering of an experience a child has had. All children—whether abused or not—have fantasies about their own and their parents' sexuality. These can be misunderstood or assessed incorrectly by individuals not trained to understand children and their play (see p. 88n, below). A recent epidemic of alleged sexual abuse of children by adults in England led to the establishment of a royal commission, which recommended the following:

> Anatomically correct dolls are often used in the assessment of suspected sexual abuse. They are used by trained professionals as well as, unfortunately, those who are not trained to use them. They should not be used without an understanding of child development, play, fantasizing and psychopathology.
>
> They should certainly not be used as the first stage method of evaluation. . . . In our view there are too many questions concerning the validity and reliability of anatomically correct dolls to recommend their use.*

If a child has been physically or sexually assaulted (so that the child's life or physical safety is threatened), the presumption is that the child must be assured of being in a safer environment. An exception to removing the child may be warranted if the factors that caused the abuse can be identified and the parents are able to make changes or use services that will prevent a recurrence.

*Report of the Inquiry into Child Abuse in Cleveland, England, 1987. Presented to the Parliament by the Secretary of State for Social Services by Command of Her Majesty, July, 1988.

The following are cases of sexual abuse in which the efforts of CPS workers and child psychiatrists were combined to determine the least detrimental alternative for the children involved.

CASE 17

Emily and siblings. Flagrant sexual abuse. Abusers known. Children permanently placed.

Emily lived with her mother, stepfather, and three younger half-siblings, Teresa, Mike, and Owen Berea. Her biological father was unknown. When Emily was 11 years old, her mother left Mr. Berea, taking Emily with her. Mrs. Berea relinquished custody of her three younger children to their father. She lived with several men, all heavy drinkers like herself, but returned sporadically to Mr. Berea after he suffered a heart attack. When Teresa was almost 11 and Mike and Owen almost 10 and 8, Mrs. Berea left for good, taking only Emily, then 14, with her. She ultimately moved in with another man, also an alcoholic.

Twice during the following year, Emily appealed for help, once to her stepfather and once to CPS, alleging that her mother and her mother's companion had involved her repeatedly in their sexual activities. Mrs. Berea and the man were arrested, pleaded guilty to charges of risk of injury to a minor and sexual assault, and were incarcerated. Emily was placed in a long-term foster home.

After Mr. Berea's death two years later following a second heart attack, CPS obtained temporary custody of his children and placed Teresa and Mike in one foster home and Owen in another. (Unfortunately no placement was available where the three children could be together.) The children feared that their mother, when released from prison, would succeed in her intentions to regain custody of them and marry her boyfriend. More than likely Teresa, if not her brothers, had learned from Emily that Mrs. Berea and her boyfriend had exploited her sexually while she was in their care. The foster parents reported steady improvement in the children, and after nineteen months they were clearly thriving in their new homes, which offered affection and protection. Mrs. Berea did not arrange to see her children at all while she was incarcerated. She visited with them only occasionally after her release, and in the months that followed she failed to maintain contact. She chose to remain with her boyfriend.

When CPS moved to terminate her parental rights, Mrs. Berea asserted that she wanted frequent visitation privileges and the return of the children to her and her boyfriend at some point in the coming year. A child psychiatrist was asked by the Superior Court for Juvenile Matters to carry out a clinical evaluation to assist the court in deciding about the petition for parental rights. Based on interviews with the biological mother, the foster parents, and the children, and on interactions between the children and the respective adults, the psychiatrist wrote: "There is no question about the unreliability of the mother, who now wants to persuade [the children] to overlook the neglect and maltreatment to which she subjected them for years. The three children for whose destinies Mrs. Berea now seeks to assume responsibility are acutely aware that she was not even able to afford their older half-sister the most elementary protection against her own and her companion's abusive sexual behavior."

To assure the children of the best placement, keeping in mind that Mrs. Berea had abused Emily and abandoned the other children, the psychiatrist further stated: "We also believe that Mrs. Berea should not participate in the children's lives in any way at the present time. Their ties with her should be severed. If the question of resuming some kind of contact with her should arise at a later date, it would best be resolved by the children and their permanent caretakers at such time."

Considerations in this case:

1. A mother and her boyfriend repeatedly sexually abused her daughter, who asked for help. This child could never again live with her mother.

2. However, an evaluation was needed to spell out alternative placements for the mother's remaining children once it was clear that the mother had abandoned them. It was also necessary to determine whether she ever could provide them with a safe and nurturing environment, even though she had never directly abused them.

3. The evaluation revealed that this mother had chosen the boyfriend over her children.

4. The principle of the least detrimental alternative—that is, the termination of parental rights—should have been carried out much earlier. Unfortunately, legal and bureaucratic procedures favored the adults to the severe detriment of the children.

CASE 18

Chuck and May. Abusers strongly suspected; recommendation that children be removed.

Chuck and May Mantrel, ages 7 and 6, were placed in foster care at their mother's request when she was hospitalized for one of six suicide attempts. There had been repeated instances of neglect and endangerment when the children lived with their mother. The children often were left alone. When there was food in the house—not always the case—Chuck did much of the cooking. Their living arrangements were precarious and chaotic. At times they slept in police stations, in the street or the woods, or on someone's floor. The children also had been physically abused, tied to the furniture for punishment or beaten with metal spoons, spatulas, and belts. They had been hospitalized for accidental burns and the ingestion of drugs. Petitions of neglect, abuse, or abandonment were filed by CPS.

Six months after the first placement, the children were legally committed to CPS. Because of the severity of their emotional distress, they were moved to a therapeutic foster home. Chuck was hyperactive, aggressive, confused, and often withdrew into fantasy. He was subject to nightmares and temper tantrums and

smeared feces on himself. May, chronically encopretic and enu-
retic, was inhibited, manipulative, easily distracted, and talked
compulsively. Psychiatric treatment was initiated.

With ongoing treatment and the increased security and trust
derived from their new foster placement, the children became less
symptomatic. They had started to reveal, both to their therapists
and to their foster mother, many past instances of large group
sexual activity initiated by their father. This man had a criminal
record, had lived with the family only sporadically, and had disappeared when May and Chuck were 5 and 6 years old. The alleged sexual abuse had included fondling, molestation, and vaginal
and rectal intercourse and had involved many other adults as well
as several neighborhood children. Although the mother pleaded
ignorance, there was evidence that she had been, at times, aware
of these activities and probably an occasional participant in them.
The children's foster mother and therapists found this information, though not verifiable, to be both convincing and credible and
consistent with the play therapy and the drawings produced by
both Chuck and May.*

CPS filed a recommendation in court that the children be
placed permanently and freed for adoption. To the intense frustration of the CPS worker, several witnesses at the last moment
changed their testimony. As a result, rather than granting a petition for termination of parental rights, the judge recommended
yet another referral for psychiatric treatment of the children and
the mother, the purpose of which would be to work toward the
return of the children to their mother.

Two child experts, upon receiving this referral, informed CPS
of their unwillingness to cooperate with the court-ordered treatment plan. They wrote:

---

*To consider a child's play and drawings as evidence, in a legal sense, of
what has happened to a child is incorrect. Instead, these complex phenomena
reflect such things as a child's imagination, fantasies, conflicts, and life experiences, as well as developmental level and intelligence.

It is our opinion that at this time it is critical for both Chuck and May to have a permanent placement. The most harmful situation for the children is one in which uncertainty is perpetuated. We believe it would be in the children's best interest for the court to request an evaluation conducted by a child psychiatrist which would focus on the quality of the children's relationship to their biological mother and whether they can ever again establish a trusting relationship with her.

The children have consistently divulged information indicating that they were subjected to many forms of sexual assault and exploitation. It is our opinion that such allegations require careful assessment to determine whether the children's ability to trust in and feel protected by the parent has been irreparably impaired. Since placement, both children reportedly have articulated their wish not to return to their mother's care.

Until the issue of placement is resolved, we believe that another therapeutic intervention involving the children and their mother would not be in their best interest because it would only serve to delay a permanent plan for them and could in fact undermine some of the gains the children have made since placement. In addition, such a use of therapy often serves to interfere with children's ability to feel confidence in psychiatric treatment.

As a result of this written protest, CPS was able to proceed with the termination of parental rights, which ultimately was granted, and the children were adopted.

Considerations in this case:

1. Although CPS recommended termination of parental rights, the judge initially did not concur.

2. Had a court-appointed child expert been involved in evaluating the case sooner, it is possible that the matter would have

been settled more promptly in favor of the children and a more timely plan for placement and treatment implemented.

3. When treatment is used by the court as an alternative to the resolution of a placement problem, it often becomes a delaying and undermining action.

4. This case raises an issue that may appear in subtle and disguised ways. That is, when professionals try to delay the placement decision, are they avoiding the principle of the least detrimental alternative? Under many circumstances, treatment neither provides relief nor improves the available alternatives for placement.

CASE 19

Louise. Sexual abuse. Abuser known in one instance.

The subject of this case was abused sexually at age 6, once by a known assailant and a second time in a manner that has remained a mystery.

For her first six years, Louise Morse lived with her mother and two older brothers. While visiting her grandmother, she was raped by a 15-year-old neighborhood boy whom the family did not know. (He subsequently was caught and arrested.) She was hospitalized for several days, enrolled in a sexual-trauma treatment program, and recommended for psychotherapy. For undetermined reasons, however, Ms. Morse did not follow through on these recommendations for her daughter and declined to permit any further evaluation.

Five months later, when she was almost 7, Louise was again assaulted sexually, this time while visiting her maternal aunt with her mother and siblings. The examining gynecologist found that Louise had a vaginal laceration and bleeding. The gynecologist thought that the laceration had been caused by a hard sharp object and not by a penis, but the cause of the injury never was determined. Louise remained hospitalized for more than a week. To those working on the case Ms. Morse appeared defensive and un-cooperative. An Order of Temporary Custody was obtained by CPS, and after two brief placements Louise moved to the home of her foster mother, Mrs. Acacia.

Following Louise's second trauma, communications deterio-rated between Ms. Morse and all others involved with her daugh-ter. Correctly or not, Ms. Morse's belligerence and secretiveness were perceived by CPS workers as suggestive of guilt rather than of the wish to keep Louise in her care.

Therapy was recommended for both Louise and her mother.

Louise began treatment, but her mother, despite reassurances of confidentiality, decided against it for herself. She feared that what she told the professional might be conveyed to CPS and used against her. Reassurances by CPS that she could see a therapist of her choice were to no avail.

Ms. Morse and the foster mother were not compatible, and Ms. Morse stopped visiting her daughter six weeks after Louise moved in with Mrs. Acacia. On the day that CPS obtained commitment of Louise, the mother abducted her daughter as she was returning from school. The child, whose whereabouts then became un-known, was located through school authorities in Vermont and returned to the Acacia home after a two-and-a-half month absence. Since Ms. Morse remained silent, the only information available about this interlude came from Louise, who claimed that her mother had tied her up and beaten her with a belt when she ex-pressed the wish to return to her foster family.

In the months that followed, CPS wrote six times to Ms. Morse by registered mail, encouraging her to come to Connecticut to visit her daughter. When she did return nine months later and asked to see Louise, then almost 9 years old, CPS questioned whether this visit was in the girl's best interest. The issue was brought before the court, and the help of a child psychiatrist was sought to eval-uate the visitation and placement issues. On the basis of many records, especially individual and joint interviews conducted with Louise, her mother, and her foster mother, the psychiatrist reached the following conclusions:

a. An assessment of Louise's relationship to her mother and foster mother shows that she has a significant psychological relationship with both of these adults, but that with Mrs. Acacia is seen as the more positive. Louise is obviously comfortable with the Acacias and their grandchildren. For whatever reasons, and facts are scanty, she is afraid of her mother and claims she is an abuser. Whether in fact Ms. Morse has abused her, we do not know.

b. As to the developmental gains Louise has made while with Mrs. Acacia, there is ample documentation from school and the therapist that she has made good progress. Because of her fear of her mother and the fear that she will again be taken from Mrs. Acacia, some regression should be expected if her mother becomes reinvolved.

c. Whether psychological damage will occur if Louise has renewed contact with her mother is impossible for me to predict. We know the mother is very secretive about her own life. This makes it extremely difficult to know to what sort of environment Louise would return.

d. As for the advisability of renewed visitation between Louise and her mother, I believe it is worth the risk. I believe if Ms. Morse knew better how to use "The System," was not so secretive, and did not so quickly antagonize people, Louise would probably never have been taken away. The fact is, however, that Louise has now found a supportive home with the Acacias, and she wants to stay.

Appropriate visitation is a way of deciding more definitively what her best permanent placement should be. While visitation will frighten her and perhaps cause some psychological burden, the burden of separation from one's biological mother and the self-recriminations that might follow in the future demand that cutting mother off from daughter not be done too quickly. Ms. Morse did raise Louise for almost seven years and it is Ms. Morse's family that Louise draws as her own. [In response to the psychiatrist's request during an interview that the child "draw a family."]

e. If visitation does take place, it should be in a "neutral" setting. I suggest there be present an observer who is neutral in this case and who has experience with parent-child interactions. If Louise becomes increasingly comfortable with her mother during hour-long, twice weekly visits, there can be longer and more private contacts. On the other hand, if Louise does not get over her fears after two months or her psychological state begins to deteriorate, it will be clear that contact is better avoided.

f. I recommend that permanent planning occur after obtaining the findings that will result from the above.

Considerations in this case:

1. A child psychiatrist weighed the advantages and disadvantages for a sexually abused child of maintaining a relationship with her biological mother, who presumably had not adequately protected her child.

2. This psychiatrist deferred any recommendation that the child's ties to her biological mother be severed entirely. Instead, he recommended conducting an experiment in which visits with her mother in a safe setting would be used as the determining factor in deciding whether the child should be returned to her biological mother or freed for adoption. This type of experiment is usually unsuccessful because it does not adequately represent the child's behavior and further postpones making a decision based on the least detrimental alternative. This postponement may be damaging in itself because it further undermines the child's confidence in the adults who are responsible for her or his care.

3. The inability of the state and of the experts to recommend the least detrimental alternative in a clear and decisive manner un-

doubtedly contributed to the further difficulties experienced by this child.

Follow-up:

Unfortunately, Louise's next years continued on a confused course. When she was 9 years old, CPS filed for termination of her mother's parental rights. This was granted, an action that Ms. Morse appealed. Louise reportedly experienced much anxiety during this time, stating her wish to be adopted by Mrs. Acacia.

The following year, Louise ran away from the home of her foster family to that of an aunt, where she spent three months. She then was placed in a series of shelters for the next eight months, during which time the state Supreme Court overturned the termination ruling. At the request of Louise and Ms. Morse, visits began later that year and continued on weekends and holidays through the balance of the school year without any known negative consequences. At the age of 11, Louise was returned to her mother's care. Ms. Morse was cautiously cooperative with CPS.

Discussion:

Louise had been traumatized physically and sexually and was apparently unable to form a primary psychological relationship either with her mother or with the foster mother. In retrospect, the least detrimental alternative would have been to terminate parental rights and free the child for adoption.

CASE 20

Rose. Sexual abuse of adolescent girl by father. Recommendation that father be removed from home.

When Rose Hawkins was 9 years old, CPS learned that her 18-year-old sister, Adele (by then living away from home), had been involved in an incestuous relationship with her father for the past decade. The mother had known about this and was "revolted," but had taken no action. The entire family was referred to a child guidance clinic, where both parents attended therapy sessions. Rose was seen on a weekly basis. The clinic staff believed that "several positive gains had been established and that Rose appeared to be better protected within the family." Her therapist wrote that she had "strengthened Rose's chain of support in the event of incestuous problems." CPS closed the case within the year.

Four years later, when Rose was 13, the case was reopened when a friend of hers told an anonymous reporter that Rose was being sexually abused by her father. Rose later confided during an evaluation that her father had touched her breasts and genital area on a few occasions over a four-month period. She denied that sexual penetration had occurred or that her father had coerced her in any way.

The mother refused to bring charges against the father. CPS realized that she would not protect the child from her father, nor would the father agree to leave the home. The least detrimental alternative available to CPS, therefore, was to obtain an Order of Temporary Custody on the basis of neglect and to place Rose in foster care. In conjunction with a petition to commit Rose to CPS, a child psychiatrist conducted a court-ordered evaluation of Rose and her family.

Rose had a good experience with her foster family for seven months, during which time she maintained contact with her biological family in supervised visits. Although in some ways angry with them for both their actions and their inactions, Rose missed them and wished to live at home. Having pleaded guilty to the charge of reckless endangerment of a minor, Mr. Hawkins was incarcerated. In a separate court-ordered evaluation, he was found to be clinically depressed. He felt ashamed and guilty about what had happened.

In a follow-up assessment, the child psychiatrist recommended that Rose be returned to her mother and that she and her mother both enter therapy—Rose for help in dealing with her feelings related to the sexual issues and Mrs. Hawkins for help in understanding her inability to act more constructively to resolve family problems.

Rose was strongly attached to her mother. Although Mrs. Hawkins felt immobilized, the evaluator believed that her unresponsiveness to the clues she had perceived probably stemmed from an intense need to avoid the threat of separation from her husband. The psychiatrist wrote: "When Mr. Hawkins is ready for parole, there should be an assessment of both his and the child's emotional state and the mother's capacity to protect Rose and to assist in determining whether Mr. Hawkins can return to the family or live apart from them."

Considerations in this case:

1. This recommendation conformed to the principle that the child must be safeguarded by separating the adult suspected of committing the assault from the child.

2. Because the mother would not confirm the allegation that the father had molested his younger adolescent daughter, and because the father insisted on remaining at home, CPS sought legal custody on the basis of neglect and initially placed the adolescent with a foster family. Once the father was incarcerated, the girl could safely return home.

3. Teenage girls who have been sexually molested by a member of the family often have a strong need to be reunited with their mothers, even when the mothers have failed to protect them adequately. In such instances, the need for safety must be weighed against the daughter's developmental need and wish to remain or return home.

Follow-up:

At the recommendation of a family counselor at the Veterans Administration and of the psychiatrist who had assessed Rose, Mr. Hawkins returned home, having served a sixteen-month prison sentence. Six months later, the case was closed. When Rose was 17, she married and gave birth to a child.

CASE 21

Daphne. Sexual abuse by stepfather. Illustration of adolescent girl's strong need for mother.

When Daphne Colak was 8 years old, her parents were divorced and her mother married Mr. Sanders, by whom she had become pregnant. Daphne and her brother Burt, age 12, resented their stepfather, a harsh disciplinarian, whose behavior was supported by their mother.

Four years later, Burt Colak became a management problem. Unable to get along with his stepfather, at his mother's request and with the help of CPS, the 16-year-old was placed in a residential treatment center. While there, Burt divulged several instances of sexual abuse involving his stepfather and his sister, as well as himself and his stepfather. The staff reported the abuse to the police. Mr. Sanders was arrested, convicted of sexual assault, and after one month's incarceration received a suspended sentence.

Although it seemed clear that Mrs. Sanders had been aware of these sexual activities (Daphne claimed to have told her about them), the CPS worker reported that "she denied the incest and/or its impact on Daphne. In her emotional turmoil, she became a dysfunctional parent." Furthermore, she chose to have Mr. Sanders remain with her despite the risk to her children. One year later, legal charges were brought against Mr. Sanders for sexual abuse of a nonfamily member, and he again was incarcerated. At this time, Daphne, then 13, directly acknowledged to a CPS worker that her stepfather had abused her. Daphne was adjudicated as neglected and abused, committed to CPS, and placed in a foster home. Her adjustment in the foster family was good, but she continued to demonstrate a strong attachment to her own family. There were frequent telephone calls and visits, and she often expressed a longing to be back home with her mother and two younger brothers.

As part of a court-ordered evaluation, a child psychiatrist made an assessment. He noted in his report:

> While Daphne is happy in her foster home and with her foster family, she wants to be back with her mother and siblings. She knows that her mother does not want to give up

Mr. Sanders, and avoids addressing her own feelings about him. Daphne would like to live with her mother even if Mr. Sanders is there and recognizes that, if mother is forced to choose, she very likely would continue to place Mr. Sanders first and Daphne's safety, second. Despite this realization, Daphne wishes to return to her mother's care.

We do not perceive that either mother or stepfather act in any intentionally malicious or harmful way. However, their individual pathology does intrude in a negative and destructive way in the lives of their children. Mrs. Sanders' own needs for attention and love are so intensely preoccupying that she has been and remains unable to meet the needs of her children for protection.

While we recognize that Daphne wants to return home, it would not be safe for her to do so at this time. She should continue to live in her foster home for now.

A court-ordered evaluation by the same psychiatrist two years later updated his findings with the observation that Daphne should be gradually reunited with her mother and siblings. This recommendation was based on Daphne's communication of an urgent need to be reunited with her mother. Daphne, by then almost 16 years old, took her fate into her own hands, ran away from the foster home, and returned herself to her mother's care.

Considerations in this case:

1. This case depicts the powerful need of an adolescent girl for her mother, despite her mother's inability to protect her and her refusal to extrude the abusing husband.

2. The tendency to remove the child, rather than the sexually exploitative adult, exposes the child to a double injury—that is, both sexual abuse and banishment from the home and the parent she needs. If the mother cannot protect the daughter from illicit visits by the abusing father, however, the daughter's safety requires that she be placed elsewhere.

Follow-up:

Soon after Daphne's sixteenth birthday CPS closed her case. Two years later her situation was unknown, except that she was no longer living with her mother, who had made "other arrangements" for her.

CASE 22

Ellen and Larry. Unconfirmed accusation of parents as sexual abusers.

In this case two children were removed from their home on a ninety-six-hour hold. The following circumstances led to an unwarranted and harmful intrusion.

Jenny Pulaski, aged 5, reported both to her parents and to her therapist that she had been sexually abused by her neighbor Larry Larousse, the 16-year-old brother of her friend Ellen. Jenny further stated that some months earlier, while she was visiting Ellen, the Larousses had initiated sexually oriented games, including one called "drop the panties." She claimed that the participants had been photographed in varying stages of nudity by Mrs. Larousse, whose Polaroid camera developed the pictures on the spot.

Jenny's parents notified CPS and stated their intent to press charges against Larry. Jenny's therapist also filed a report both to CPS and to the local police department that contained similar allegations. In his report the therapist expressed his opinion that "5-year-olds do not lie or make up stories about sexual abuse." Upon learning about the complaint of sexual molestation against Larry, the Larousses arranged for him to enter treatment. In the context of this treatment, it became clear that Larry had also played sexually with his sister.

Shortly after the referral to CPS, the police appeared unannounced with a warrant to search the Larousse home. The Larousses were outraged. The police confiscated two cameras and photograph albums, under the suspicion that they contained pictures of indecent exposure, but nothing of this nature was found. The Larousses at the time of the alleged "games" had not, in fact, possessed a Polaroid camera. They vehemently denied all the allegations against them.

Charges of risk of injury to a minor were brought against the Larousses by CPS, and Larry and Ellen were removed from the home by the police and the CPS worker. The worker, having obtained a ninety-six-hour hold, placed Ellen in an emergency shelter. Because she was so young, she was assigned to a room with a guard at the door, "to protect the child from abuse and neglect and to provide a temporary safe environment for her." After four days, Ellen was released to the home of her maternal aunt; five days later, the court returned her to her parents' home. Larry, who had spent four days in another shelter, was released to his maternal grandparents on the condition that he have no further contact with his sister.

As part of the court proceedings, the judge requested psychiatric assessments of both Larry and Ellen, as well as psychological evaluations of the children and their parents, their relationships with each other, and the parents' ability to care for the children. During this evaluation, Mr. and Mrs. Larousse denied all claims of improper conduct on their part. Their cameras and albums were returned by the police, who found nothing to confirm Jenny's allegations.

Mr. and Mrs. Larousse appeared to be distressed by the events of the previous two months. They felt that their personal lives had been invaded and disrupted by the accusations made against them, by the police raid on their home, and by the abrupt removal of their children. Ellen in turn worried that someone would come to her school and take her away, or that a stranger would come into the house and remove her. She was also afraid that her parents would not protect her from such intrusions and was angry with them for having allowed the worker to take her away from home.

Ellen at this time was a fragile, disorganized girl, severely anxious and depressed. The trauma of the abrupt and frightening removal and subsequent nine-day separation from her parents disrupted her development. A child of Ellen's age depends on her parents to be in control of her safety and well-being. Ellen was angry at her parents for their inability to protect her from being taken away from their care. She also felt guilty about the sexual play with her brother, and she perceived the enforced separation as punitive. She was upset and angry with her parents and others in authority whom she felt had inflicted a cruel punishment on her.

Considerations in this case:

1. The intervention by the state violated several principles:

a) This case met none of the Guidelines' criteria listed either under "Emergency or Immediate Removal (for 96 Hours or Less—Temporary Hold)" or under "Planned Removal."*

b) The intake worker did not make an initial assessment of the parents and child(ren). The Guidelines state that "assessments should involve the least disturbing and most constructive individual consideration of each parent and child." There was no "careful investigation" to determine whether the conditions necessitated the children's removal from home. As the Guidelines further state, "Case workers should examine *how* the sexual relationship occurred as well as *that it did*." In this instance, the worker overreacted to the statements made by a 5-year-old neighbor to her parents and to her therapist; the "careful investigation" that occurred much later strongly suggested that this child's allegations were based largely on her own fantasies rather than on facts.†

2. A precipitous removal, far from assuring a 5-year-old child "of being in a safer environment," had the opposite effect. Her four days and nights in an inappropriate emergency shelter instead traumatized her and undermined her trust in her parents.

---

*See appendix 1.

†We are currently living in a period of hysteria, in which it is alleged that children always tell the factual truth, even when they do not understand the concept of truth.

3. Sexual play between the siblings, aged 16 and 5, could have warranted a referral for evaluation and treatment. The drastic steps that were taken were disproportionate to the situation and created suffering for all members of the family, the long-term effects of which still are to be determined.

Co-terminous Petition—Life-Threatening Injury

This concept is guided by the presumption that children who have been placed outside of their homes because of life-threatening injuries at the hands of the adults responsible for them should not be returned to those adults. Such children will never feel emotionally secure with the adults who attacked them.* The CPS should file co-terminous petitions for these children.

Workers often find it difficult, however, to proceed with the co-terminous petition. The worker sometimes identifies with the parents, resulting in his or her conviction that the termination petition is unduly unfair or punitive to them. As one worker put it, "I can't do this. It would be like killing the parents." Furthermore, when the life of a child is threatened, workers often find themselves caught in a dilemma: they are responsible not only for the safety of the child but also for the rehabilitation of the parents. The finality of the idea that it is too late for a parent to be rehabilitated for a particular child—although rehabilitation might be feasible for future children—can be difficult to tolerate.

A variety of complex factors may be at play in the worker's reluctance or delay in filing the co-terminous petition. Denial sometimes arises when the worker must confront the abhorrent fact that an adult, especially a parent, would injure or attempt to kill a child. Some workers have a strong bias against termination of parental rights because of religious, philosophical, or cultural beliefs that children should not be taken away from their parents. Other workers fear being humiliated, embarrassed, or defeated by

*See appendix 1.

the court's response to such a petition. There are several other less obvious areas of difficulty: there may be conflict between worker and supervisor as to whether the termination of parental rights is justified,* or workers may feel that they do not have the time to compile, or data to substantiate, a petition that would justify this drastic court action. Further, the role of the state's lawyer is ambiguous. Does he or she primarily serve the best interests of the state, or primarily the best interests of the child who is a ward of the state? Ordinarily the state's attorney serves the best interests of the state even if they are different from or in conflict with the best interests of the child. In such instances it is realistic and appropriate to appoint or activate an independent legal counsel for the child, as is required in Connecticut.

The worker, however, is responsible for filing such a coterminous petition. It is then the responsibility of the court to validate or overcome the presumption that the child should not be returned to the original caretaker. The judge makes the final decision.

The subsequent development of a child of any age who has suffered a life-threatening injury at the hands of his caretakers would be seriously jeopardized if the child were to be raised by those who were responsible for the injury. The risk is both a physical and an emotional one that is neither consistent with the best interests of the child nor in keeping with the least detrimental alternative.

Skeptics who wonder if young children really can remember such traumatic events often ask why children cannot be returned to their biological parents once sufficient intervention has been provided to ensure their future physical safety. Clinical experience indicates that each child inevitably gains an awareness or a sense

---

*It is our impression that the more closely the supervisor is involved in planning for the child, the more likely he or she is to feel convinced that termination of parental rights in these cases is necessary.

that an injury has occurred—whether through actual memory, through clues furnished by scars or impairments, or through subtler communications from individuals who perpetrated, witnessed, or knew about the injury. Such children experience the injury either as a damaging burden to be remembered and reconstructed time and again or as one to be warded off by repeated attempts to forget. Being cared for by adults who have not jeopardized the child's life or physical integrity, and who are loving and nurturing, facilitates his or her efforts to overcome and master the trauma. The presumption that the child will not be returned is less detrimental than the assumption that "if you can't remember what happened, it won't hurt you."

In the following cases CPS workers decided to file co-terminous petitions.*

CASE 23

Olivia. Co-terminous petition associated with life-threatening injuries, presumably at hands of parents.

In this case a co-terminous petition was filed by CPS and contested by the parents. Commitment and termination of parental rights were sought because Olivia, while in the care of her biological parents, was seriously injured twice.

Olivia was born prematurely in Hawaii and spent her first three weeks in the hospital. At 7 months, with her parents and 2-year-old sister, she moved to the West Coast to live with cousins. A year later, a brother was born. Soon after this, all of the Kaluas (father, mother, and two siblings) except Olivia, then 20 months old, moved east, where the parents were to receive special job training. During that period, for reasons that remain unclear, Olivia was left in the cousins' care. When Olivia was just 2 years old, Mr. Kalua abruptly took her from the cousins' home, a separation that caused the child great distress.

At 25 months, Olivia was hospitalized with a subdural hema-

*See Cases 1 and 2 for other co-terminous petitions.

toma, a fractured arm, a healing fracture of the other arm, and numerous bruises. The parents offered no explanation for these injuries, other than that Olivia had fallen from a sofa. During the hospitalization, the child was observed to be unusually quiet, even in the presence of her parents. CPS obtained an Order of Temporary Custody, and Olivia was discharged to a foster family for three weeks, after which she was returned to her home under "protective supervision." Three months later the case was closed.

Nine months after the original series of injuries, when Olivia was almost 3, she was again hospitalized, this time for a ruptured spleen, severe pancreatitis and dehydration, shock, and multiple bruises. On this occasion, the parents blamed her 22-month-old brother, who they claimed had literally sat on her, an explanation the doctors were unable to accept. Olivia's recovery in the hospital was slow. She appeared sad, withdrawn, or frightened much of the time, including when she was in the presence of her biological parents. Six weeks later, she was discharged to a long-term foster home, in which she has remained. A co-terminous petition was filed after the second hospitalization.

A court-ordered evaluation was performed collaboratively by a child psychiatrist and a pediatrician who was also a specialist in child development. The evaluation was based on extended observation of Olivia in the hospital, a developmental examination, observations of Olivia with both her foster and her biological parents and siblings, and two joint interviews with Mr. and Mrs. Kalua. The contrast between Olivia's appearance and behavior in the presence of her foster family and her biological family was striking. With the former, she was happy, animated, and imaginative; with her biological family, both in and out of the hospital, she seemed immobilized, anxious, and wary. The evaluators noted that the child "showed not only lack of positive feelings, but severe negative ones—anxiety and fear."

Both parents adamantly denied any responsibility for Olivia's various injuries, which they maintained were the result of separate and essentially unpreventable accidents. The evaluators found the parents to have no overt psychiatric or behavioral disorders but were impressed by their apparent obliviousness to the seriousness of their daughter's injuries.

The experts recommended that Olivia not be returned to her biological parents. To do so would be to risk her life or jeopardize the continuation of her good development. "Her marked anxiety suggests that she remembers and is terrified of further hurt. It seems unlikely that she ever could trust or be comfortable or happy with parents who have not protected her from such severe trauma. A return would be terrifying for her."

Considerations in this case:

1. This child suffered life-threatening injuries while in the care of her parents. The presumption must be that one or both parents physically abused the child, who could never again feel secure with them.

2. A co-terminous petition should have been filed at the time of the first hospitalization, since the child's initial injuries were life threatening.

CASE 24

Carol. Petition associated with injuries inflicted on an infant before her third month of life.

The co-terminous petition filed by CPS for Carol Joslin, hospitalized at 6 weeks of age with multiple injuries, was contested by Ms. Marlov, her 36-year-old mother. Ms. Marlov's first baby, born when she was 18 years old, was released for adoption at birth. Ms. Marlov said that as the father "didn't want to be bothered" and as she could not then care for a child, she had had "no problem" with this decision.

Ms. Marlov's next relationship, entered into when she was 24 and lasting intermittently for ten years, was a stormy one. She became pregnant but had an abortion "to try to save the relationship," the father being adamant in not wanting the child. Shortly after this event the couple married, but allegedly owing to her husband's repeated infidelity, they divorced seven years later.

Ms. Marlov's next alliance, with Mr. Joslin, led to the conception of Carol; after several weeks of indecision, she decided not to abort this pregnancy. Mr. Joslin's work problems, together with Ms. Marlov's difficult pregnancy and slow recovery from a complicated delivery, exacerbated an already deteriorating relationship. The couple entered into counseling. After Carol's birth, Ms. Marlov contacted Parents Anonymous and programmed the number of a Care Line into their telephone because counselors were alarmed by Mr. Joslin's expressed hostility toward the baby.

When Carol was 6 weeks old, specialists discovered that she had multiple fractures in widely different stages of healing; these injuries were judged to have been inflicted since her birth. Specifically, she had three separate skull fractures, a subdural effusion, a right radial fracture, a left femur fracture, left and right tibial fractures, and a fractured rib. After the insertion of two subdural peritoneal shunts, her condition improved and one month later she was discharged to a foster home.

Mr. Joslin described and demonstrated both to a hospital social worker and to the judge how he had squeezed, shaken, and dropped the baby. He subsequently was arrested and went to prison. In a court-ordered evaluation, Ms. Marlov admitted to having heard Mr. Joslin threaten to hurt Carol, but was "in a fog. I was not concentrating." Although Mr. Joslin once told her that he had given Carol a "bloody nose," she denied any concern that he had been abusing the baby. The day before Carol's hospitalization Mr. Joslin had told Ms. Marlov, "I squeezed Carol," but she recounted that the baby had "looked fine." That afternoon, noticing bruises on Carol's back, Ms. Marlov called the Care Line, but on being questioned about Mr. Joslin and advised to have "Carol checked immediately," she failed to do so on the grounds that the person on the telephone had "overreacted, panicked."

As ordered by the court, a psychiatrist met with Ms. Marlov

on three occasions, once with the baby, with whom her interactions appeared to be entirely appropriate. Psychological testing found Ms. Marlov to be of average intelligence, without organic impairment, depressed, but without a thought disorder. The psychiatrist's clinical impressions were consistent with the results of the psychological testing. The psychiatrist found Ms. Marlov to be apathetic about traumatic events from her past. She showed no feeling, for example, when she described her mother's death, rejection by her father, and six subsequent years in foster homes. She also displayed no emotion about Mr. Joslin's assaults on her daughter. Although able to describe in detail the injuries that he had inflicted, she said: "When I start getting angry about what Sam did, I try to remind myself that he needs my prayers. I know Sam, and the person I know couldn't have meant to hurt Carol. I hope that some day Carol gets to know her father. I think she has a right to. Sam never knew his father. I can't picture refusing Carol being with Sam after he gets some help. I don't believe Sam would ever hurt Carol intentionally." The psychiatrist observed that Ms. Marlov's continuing focus on Mr. Joslin demonstrated her greater concern for him than for her brutalized daughter. To quote from the psychiatrist's letter to the judge:

> When Ms. Marlov was asked very directly how her lack of anger toward her daughter's assailant might endanger Carol in the future, she had no answer. Instead, she repeated, "I don't dwell on these things. There's nothing I can do about the past."

> The life-threatening and chronic nature of Carol's multiple injuries demonstrates that Mr. Joslin's assaults were persistent and severely damaging to Carol. Although Ms. Marlov lived with Carol and Mr. Joslin, she was never sufficiently aware of these ongoing physical assaults to take remedial action to protect Carol. She was completely unable to mobilize appropriate anger towards any hurtful person in

her life, including the man who so brutally assaulted her daughter. She appeared oblivious to the danger to her daughter. Ms. Marlov's lifelong pattern of denial of her angry feelings, combined with such denial in the face of life-threatening danger to her daughter, raises very serious concerns about Carol's safety in her custody. She is at risk of being murderously assaulted once again if she is returned to Ms. Marlov's custody. I therefore recommend that Carol be freed for adoption as rapidly as possible so that she can have an opportunity to be raised in a safe, nurturing home.

Considerations in this case:

1. This mother can be viewed as a passive lethal agent in the child's life. The child's repeated experience of life-threatening injuries in her presence indicated an immediate need for a co-terminous petition.

2. This case illustrates how and why decisions about removal should be based mainly on the child's injuries rather than, as often happens, on a clinical psychiatric diagnosis of the parents. In fact, the mother's ability to appear cooperative was persuasive, and experienced professionals were tempted to return the child to her.

3. Attempting to rehabilitate the mother was not realistic. The unconscionable length of time that would be required for her to become capable of caring safely for her child (if this were to prove feasible at all) would have compounded the psychological trauma already experienced by the child.

Adoption

Before presenting specific cases that deal with the issues of adoption, we will review some principles of adoption, adapted from two unpublished essays by Robert Abramovitz, "Adoption Enlightenment" and "Communicating with Children of Alternative Conception."

One of the most difficult tasks facing adoptive parents is informing their child about his or her adoption. Current adoption policy complicates this task by sustaining a variety of myths. Among them are (1) that the birth, or biological, parents retain little or no interest in their relinquished child; (2) that an adoptee's curiosity about birth parents is a sign of trouble; and (3) that reunions between adoptees and birth parents disrupt the adoptee-adopter relationship.

Current adoption laws that require agencies to seal original birth records once a child has been adopted create a conflict of interest between the birth parents, the adoptive parents, and the adoptee, known as the adoption triangle (Sorosky et al. 1978). The conflict stems from agency policies and practices that withhold information from all three parties. Although secrecy provides anonymity for the birth parents, it conflicts with the adoptee's need for information about her or his background; lack of information also may inhibit the adoptive parents' understanding of and capacity to answer the adoptee's questions. Adoptive parents should not, of course, be burdened with information that they do not wish to have.

The Role of Birth Parents

The perceived need for secrecy is buttressed by the assumption that all birth parents wish to put the adoption behind them, wanting no reminders that "they gave up their child." Interviews with many birth mothers, however, reveal that they do think about the child they bore and wish to know how the child is faring (Caplan 1990; Sorosky et al. 1978). Many birth mothers strongly prefer confidentiality; many others inquire regularly at the adoption agency about their child's welfare. Most unwed birth mothers give up their child for adoption to assure that the child will receive the love, care, and security that they themselves are not in a position to provide. These mothers often fear that they will not be forgiven for abandoning the child.

Discussions about the biological parents tend to focus on the birth mother. Reunions between adoptees and birth fathers do occur, but less is known about birth fathers. Recent studies of the unwed father reveal that he is not necessarily irresponsible and often is more concerned about the pregnancy and his offspring than has been recognized. When efforts are made to reach the biological father, his cooperation often can be obtained. Because these efforts are infrequent, however, little information about birth fathers is available to agencies.

Birth parents also often want to provide their relinquished child with additional information about their origins. This is inconsistent with the almost universal stereotype of the biological parents as impulsive or wild teenagers and adults. The desire to share information is not necessarily synonymous with a desire for reunion. Most birth parents express great appreciation for the adoptive parents' child-rearing role and do not wish to disrupt the relationship. In any case, their subsequent new lives often preclude resumption of a parental relationship with the relinquished child. Of course, increasing knowledge about the role of genetic contributions to the development and behavior of individuals makes it necessary to consider how negative genetic information should be transmitted, and by whom. If a child is born of parents with Huntington's disease or myotonic dystrophy, for example, it is important that the information be communicated.

Adoptee Curiosity

Adoptee curiosity about birth parents raises many sensitive issues. An event in the adoptee's life such as the onset of puberty, a recurrent illness, marriage, the birth of a child, or the death of an adoptive parent often triggers interest in learning about or locating the birth parent. The search usually is for information and not for a replacement relationship. In addition to discovering the biological and medical aspects of their family background, most adoptees want to know what happened to their birth parents in order to gain knowledge about themselves.

Adoptive parents may find this curiosity threatening, for they are striving to have the child feel "the same as if he/she were our own." Curiosity about or the desire to locate the birth parents often is perceived as criticism of the quality of the adoptive parent-child relationship and as a sign of ingratitude. Such insecurities stem, in part, from unresolved feelings about the inability to conceive and from an overestimation of the biological tie. When adoptive parents have confidence in their significance as the child's psychological parents, these worries are minimized. This confidence involves understanding that curiosity about the cycle of life and death and the historical continuity of the generations is normal and common; it is also evidence that adopted children trust their adoptive parents.

Children whose expressions of curiosity are met with negative or evasive responses by parents or other adult figures may become generally conflicted about "knowing" and "finding out." When adoptees sense that they do not have permission to wonder or to be curious about their origins, this may affect their attitude toward learning, as well as complicate their relationship with their adoptive parents.

Attempts to advise adoptive parents often founder because of the professionals' uncertainty concerning the conflicting issues of secrecy and openness that currently surround adoption policy. Although secrecy dominates adoption policy, it is not universal. Open adoption in selected cases has increased in recent years. In the United States, Alabama, Arizona, Connecticut, and Kansas do not have laws that require sealed records. Several European countries provide information about birth parents to adoptees. England, Wales, Scotland, Finland, and Israel permit legally emancipated adoptees to view their original birth certificates under specified conditions.

Adoptees' access to the identity of their biological parents has produced neither a rash of searches for them nor mass rejections of adoptive parents. Some adoptees are content with merely knowing that artificial barriers would not prevent them from locating their birth parents should they decide to do so. For others, the available information satisfies their need to know. Yet Robert Andersen (1988), writing from his own experience, believes that all adoptees on some level have a compelling wish to make contact with their biological families, whether or not they act on it. "The search is most fundamentally an expression of the wish to heal the wound caused by the separation . . . and to provide a more authentic base for living their lives" (p. 18).

The Enlightenment Controversy

When and how to inform a child about adoption remains controversial, complicated by the aforementioned myths and policies. The dominant view in the child welfare field favors telling a child about adoption early and often. Proponents of openness argue that secrecy can adversely affect the child's identity formation. Adoptees who "never suspected it," for example, report shock and disappointment when they accidentally discover their adoptive status. These adoptees view the adoptive parents as dishonest and untrustworthy. They may feel betrayed. The experience may also arouse feelings that the adoptive parents have been uncommunicative about other issues or have not given them permission to know what they know. Adoptees have reported growing up with a persistent feeling that "there was something I wasn't supposed to know."

Current Practices

Explaining the adoption to the child can stir up feelings in the adoptive parents about their inability to conceive, making it difficult for them to initiate the necessary discussions. In addition, when agencies withhold information about birth parents, adoptive parents often conclude that such information must have a negative significance. This can lead to persistent fantasies that their child was conceived under the worst possible circumstances and that hereditary "bad seed" influences lurk behind the secrecy shroud. Sensing that there are things they don't know or can't tell may hamper parents' attempts to be informative, which can add to the difficulty of enlightening the adopted child.

The way in which parents inform their children about adoption significantly influences how the child experiences the adoption. This therefore should be worked out carefully on an individual basis, with each set of parents and their child, in order to obtain the best resolution of the child's need to know and the parent's wish to explain it in a positive way.

Children tend to misunderstand even straightforward language. For instance, when adoptive parents tell their child "Your real mommy couldn't take care of you," the child may nevertheless misinterpret the comment as "Something was the matter with *me*, and that's why she couldn't take care of me." Similarly, children may believe that the adoptive parent is not the "real" but a "false" parent.

Recommended Parental Approach: The Role of the Agency

Once begun, the process of informing the child is a continuing one. As the child matures, he or she can master more factual information in a logical fashion free of subjective distortions. The reworking and elaboration of earlier explanations of adoption can continue to be part of the child's growing up experience without overemphasizing them. Children have different questions and different ways of expressing them, according to their developmental level.

CASE 25

Iris, Dorinda, and Andy. Threat of a disrupted adoption.

This case, other aspects of which were discussed previously,* describes the circumstances under which three siblings were adopted and how the derailment of the adoption of the oldest child was averted.

Iris, Dorinda, and Andy had been removed from their abusive mother when they were age 5, 3, and 1. Initially the children were placed separately but later in the same year were reunited in the

*See Case 9.

care of one foster family, where they appeared to thrive. The foster parents considered themselves too old to adopt the children, however, so two years later, after an intensive search, the worker came up with what under the circumstances seemed an excellent placement.

Dick and Gabrielle Johnston, married for ten years but unable to conceive a child of their own, were a hard-working couple in their early thirties. They had built, one room at a time, a twelve-room house on land they owned in the country. Having requested only one child, they were very excited at the prospect of adopting three. Gabrielle stated that their drive to build so big a house now made sense—"for the large family that [they] were meant to have."

When the children, then 7, 5, and 3 years old, arrived at the Johnstons, all had problems and were developmentally delayed. Their physical handicaps—Iris's congenital leg disorder and the younger children's osteogenesis imperfecta—required close medical supervision. At age 4 Iris had been found to have an I.Q. (Stanford-Binet) of 77. At 5½ years, her language showed a lag of one and a half to two and a half years. Her adaptive and motor functioning also were delayed. It was speculated that the child's minimal nurturing experiences and physical and emotional abuse by her biological mother had contributed significantly to this picture. Moving to another home after two years in foster placement was especially difficult for Iris.

Nevertheless, life seemed to proceed well for all three children during the early months with their new family. The parents went all out for them, as did their extended families, with such creative plans as interesting church activities and long weekends at the beach. They invested in swings, a pool, and a sandbox. Mrs. Johnston had left her job and devoted her entire day to the children. She played with them, took them on long walks, and gave fully of herself. She helped Iris every day with her schoolwork.

It was a serious blow when the formerly compliant and affectionate Iris began to turn against her adoptive mother. Increasingly disobedient and rude, she refused to cuddle with her, drew an ugly picture of her and her "yucky" hair, and hurt Mrs. Johnston's feelings. Iris also began to have behavior problems in school and would hit and swear at the other children. She continued to be affectionate with Mr. Johnston, her adoptive father; this made the already sensitive adoptive mother feel still more personally rejected.

The CPS worker was also concerned by this turn of events. Early in the placement she had made a life book for each child, and in her first visits she carefully read these books with them individually and in great detail. To her surprise, the children showed an exceptional attachment to the books and were quite possessive about them. For each child, the life book was useful in differing ways. Dorinda found her book enjoyable and interesting. Yet for Iris the book elicited, among other reactions, bitter cries for her mother. She would sob, "But why? But why? I love her. I miss her."

As a result of Iris's distress, the worker referred her to a private agency for individual psychotherapy. The agency instead insisted on family therapy in which Mr. and Mrs. Johnston and the three children were to participate. When no improvement in Iris's behavior was seen, these sessions were discontinued. The CPS worker undertook to give Mrs. Johnston guidance:

> I reassured her (and myself) that some defiance such as what Iris is displaying is normal and that Iris has not let go of her first mother yet, so understandably is resisting the idea of having a new mother. Iris never had a father, hence Dick has had no competition. Gabrielle and Dick were unsure whether they should encourage and allow Iris to talk about her past whenever she felt like it. They felt threatened and uncomfortable by her memories of the past. Dick felt Iris needed to put the past all behind her in order to make a fresh start with their family. I emphasized to them very strongly that Iris needed to talk about her past in order to work it

through and that she would feel more frustrated and troubled if she were made to keep her thoughts private.

The worker also explained to Mrs. Johnston that Iris's testing of her and questioning of her love were understandable, but that it was necessary to treat Iris and her siblings with the same degree of firmness, to reaffirm to Iris that she was loved.

Because of Iris's upsetting behavior, the CPS worker's supervisor recommended that the worker defer her individual contacts with Iris so that the children would have a chance to "settle in without reminders of their past." The girls in particular, however, had become attached to the worker during their two years in foster placement. On the worker's very next home visit, Iris approached her with, "Please, let's talk, just you and me." This presented the worker with a dilemma.

A clinical consultant advised the opposite course of action: in her opinion, Iris would benefit from more meetings with the worker, rather than fewer. The consultant believed that the best way for the child to come to terms with her grief and anger would be to express her feelings and, furthermore, that her behavior toward Mrs. Johnston most likely represented a displacement of feelings about her biological mother. It was decided that the worker should plan to meet with Iris more often and within a limited time frame. The worker agreed.

> I understood that the goal would be both to determine if there is any pathology present which needs further treatment, and to see if the issue of "letting go" can be worked out with Iris by helping her to master it through repetition. I felt ambivalence about doing this, because I was afraid I might stir up too many feelings and make her regress even more. But [the consultant] reassured me that these feelings were already stirred up by Iris's efforts to overcome past deprivation and trauma.

This plan proved to be fruitful. The worker took notes on five of these meetings.

Meeting 1. Drawing on her life book, Iris repeatedly expressed her love for her mother, stated how much she missed her, and questioned why they could not be together. The worker's answers were kind and direct, for example, "I know you love her, and she loves you. But some mommies can't take care of their babies the way they should. . . . Some mommies have problems of their own and can't do all the things for their children like they are supposed to." The worker told Iris that she and her mother would not see each other again, but that her mother knew that Iris was being cared for and that she and her siblings were all together in a nice house. "But I know this makes you sad and that you miss her," the worker added. At this, Iris, who had been sobbing, hugged the worker and volunteered other matters that had been troubling her, such as her role in a recent accident to her brother's leg. The worker added, "Your new Mommy loves you a lot, wants you to be happy, and wants to be your best friend." After expressing surprise that mothers also could be friends, Iris smiled and whispered to the worker, "I promise I will be a good girl and will be nice with my new Mommy." During the next several months, Mr. and Mrs. Johnston felt that for the first time there had been an improvement in Iris's attitude.

Meetings 2 and 3 (two and four months later). These were spent mostly in rereading the life book. When asked by the worker if she would like to write a note to her biological mother that she was well and to say goodbye to her, Iris sobbed, "I don't want to say goodbye, I want to say 'hi.'" The worker reassured her that it was all right to feel like that and that over time she would feel better. "The idea of trying to get a goodbye letter from Iris obviously did not work because she was still nowhere near ready to let go." The attempt also may have been difficult for the child because the worker unwittingly implied that she was in contact with Iris's biological mother.

Meeting 4. The worker told Iris that they would meet once a week for six to eight weeks. Iris was relieved that she would be getting all this attention and talked about the meaning of her adoption, scheduled to take place two months later.

Meeting 5. Iris spoke matter-of-factly about her biological mother and drew a picture of her new family standing together in a line. They had all taken an exhilarating trip to Disney World, followed by a lovely Christmas holiday at home.

At her adoption hearing, Iris, then 8 years old and previously inarticulate, was able to tell the judge about her past and to indicate her wish to be adopted by Mr. and Mrs. Johnston.

Considerations in this case:

1. Transitional intervention. The worker's willingness to become more, rather than less, involved with a 7-year-old child averted a situation that threatened both the child and her adoptive family.

2. Continuity. Counseling performed by a worker who already had a relationship with the child was of great value. The worker, who had offered this child friendship and understanding over many years, was in a good position to enlighten the child about her new adoptive situation. The worker's presence provided a crucial link between past and present and supported the child's ability to adjust to her new life.

3. In an important sense, by providing sufficient support for the transition process, the CPS worker was uniquely qualified to fill the state's function as temporary guardian in making a permanent placement. In addition, the worker buttressed the adoptive mother's efforts to become the child's psychological parent.

CASE 26

Tyrone. Adoption in the best interests of a 10-year-old.

This case illustrates the situation of a 10-year-old biracial child, whose best interests were judged to be served by his becoming eligible for adoption.

Tyrone Williams was born out of wedlock to a black father, aged 27, and a 21-year-old white mother. Ms. Lathe, the mother, moved out of the home with Tyrone when the baby was 2½ years old. Mr. Williams, who had physically abused both mother and son, disappeared and thereafter had no further contact with the family.

Ms. Lathe, whose drug history dated from her teens, stopped using heroin and other substances when pregnant with Tyrone but resumed regular use after his birth. In Tyrone's first five years mother and son moved several times, and Ms. Lathe held various jobs: at a travel agency, a restaurant, and a massage parlor. When Tyrone was 3, she entered a drug rehabilitation program and a second program the following year; during these periods, Tyrone was cared for by a maternal uncle. Ms. Lathe also had a boyfriend who beat the child repeatedly. CPS first became involved in the case when Tyrone was 5.

From then on Tyrone had a series of placements, interrupted by intervals of living with his mother. His first placement when 5 years old, with a white family, lasted nine months, until his mother, with legal assistance, succeeded in ending it. Committed to CPS when almost 7, Tyrone next was placed with a black couple—a teacher married to a social worker—who were friends of his maternal grandfather. Twenty months later the couple divorced, and this placement also ended. Meanwhile, Ms. Lathe had attempted to stabilize her life and was allowed another opportunity to take care of Tyrone. Within a few months, however, she had returned to drugs and could not fulfill her parental responsibilities.

After a matter of weeks with another maternal uncle and aunt (a placement that ended for indeterminate reasons) and another failed attempt for Tyrone to live with his mother, now in a third rehabilitation center, Tyrone was placed with two more foster families. When he was 10 years old, CPS filed a petition to terminate parental rights, and the court requested an expert evaluation.

The psychiatrist described Tyrone as a strikingly handsome

and appealing boy who had no serious behavior problems. He was protective of his mother, who was then in prison for embezzlement. A dark-skinned boy who considered himself white, Tyrone, despite his multiple placements, had done surprisingly well at school and in foster homes. All his placements had ended through no fault of Tyrone but because of problems within the families.

Tyrone's stated wishes were to live with his mother, his uncles, or his grandparents. He realized, however, that their homes were not available to him, although he did not understand why and wished that it were otherwise. The psychiatrist reported:

> Tyrone is a sensitive and sad youth who tries to present a cheerful appearance. The many disruptions and changes in his life seem not to have interfered with his cognitive development. He is a child who internalizes his inner distress and suffers from depression, rather than acting out his difficulties. This undoubtedly contributes to his appeal and also may be encouraging for the long-term outcome of his development and growing up. Tyrone deserves an opportunity to have a permanent home. He cannot afford to wait for his mother. He will be too old when and if she is able to be rehabilitated.
>
> We recognize that Tyrone has stated a preference for a foster placement so that he can be available to live with his mother when she is released from prison. However, he [also] told us that he wants a permanent home. . . . All talk of "permanency" [must be] unreal to this boy; indeed, he has had eight changes of placement within the last five years.
>
> Tyrone had a fantasy that he and his mother would be reunited in some idealized way and perhaps live happily-ever-after. The fantasy is understandable, as at this time, he has nothing more tangible with which to replace it.

The psychiatrist strongly recommended that Tyrone be adopted. The judge concurred.

Considerations in this case:

1. The psychiatrist's recommendation, although affirming the principle that the child's preference should be given the weight appropriate to his age and cognitive capacity, assumed that the burden and responsibility for the ultimate decision should be borne by the adults.

2. The adults' decision was that the child should be adopted, despite his manifest preference for foster placement.

3. The adoptive parents would have the authority and responsibility for deciding if and when Tyrone could be in contact with his biological mother.

Follow-up:

Five years later Tyrone was doing well in his adoptive family.

CASE 27

Roger. A biracial child in need of a home.

The case of Roger Cook describes the travails of an 11-year-old biracial child awaiting adoption. Roger's parents, a white mother and a black father, were chronic schizophrenic patients in a psychiatric hospital. Because they were considered unable to raise a child, Roger was removed from them when he was 4 days old and placed with a white foster family, the Murrays.

Roger apparently did well in his first year, but between his second and third years he stopped growing. In the course of three hospitalizations, celiac disease and failure to thrive were diagnosed as the basis for his difficulties. Also noted was a history of gorging and vomiting. When Roger was 3, a developmental examination revealed a variety of bizarre behaviors: he was withdrawn and solitary in his play; he had poor speech; and he gorged, often on dog or cat food and garbage. A psychiatric evaluation included this observation: "In Roger's fantasies, he was preoccupied with food. He played out a theme of torturing the boy doll with physical abuse and name calling. However, the main torture was food deprivation, in which the doll was tempted by watching others eat." Roger's weight and height were below the fifth percentile for his age. Two more hospital admissions before his fourth year, along with assessments of his foster family, confirmed the diagnosis of psychosocial dwarfism. At 4 years of age, Roger was placed with the Huntoons, another white family, who were thought better able to meet his emotional needs. The consultant, together with a CPS worker, noted that visits by his biological mother were disruptive, and these were discontinued. Roger showed marked improvement, both physically and socially, in this second placement. By 4 years and 2 months of age, he had experienced a dramatic growth spurt. This continued over the next several years, as recorded in follow-up examinations at six-month intervals.

At the age of 7, because of problematic school behavior, Roger was brought to a child guidance clinic for evaluation and entered into treatment with a child therapist. He was described as friendly and cooperative and of average intelligence. Psychological testing indicated that he was depressed and anxious, a key worry being the fear of abandonment by parental figures. He had few friends, claimed to be disliked because he was dark skinned, and complained that his peers called him "Darky." In therapy sessions he often spanked or fed poison to the black baby doll. These weekly meetings were discontinued after nine months, as were the Huntoons' visits with a social worker. The foster parents had resisted treatment for themselves and Roger from the outset, regarding it as an unnecessary intrusion by the state.

The following year CPS reported that Roger, now evidently an integral member of the Huntoon family, had "blossomed into a delightful youngster." Although the Huntoons did not wish to adopt him, "no home could have treated him better." They gave him love and nurturance, enrolled him in Cub Scouts and day camp, and took him on a vacation to Bermuda, where he began to become better acquainted with black culture. Roger was seen as psychologically attached to the family. This placement was considered to be a permanent foster home.

The Huntoons had invented the myth that Roger was of Spanish origin. Before Roger's tenth birthday, as a result of his questions, he was told for the first time that his father was black, his mother white, and that they both had psychiatric problems. Now both Mrs. Huntoon and the worker were being candid with him. He met often with the worker, to speak of problems and to work on his life book.

The following year Roger began to act out both at school and at home—hoarding food, lying, stealing money, and threatening to run away. This behavior escalated. As a result of his persistent requests, a meeting was arranged with his biological parents, who lived nearby—his mother with the maternal grandmother, his father in a hotel. Both parents had achieved moderate stability with supportive treatment, including a long-term relationship with a mental health center and a psychotropic drug regimen. Roger reacted positively to the meeting, evidently without adverse effects, and further meetings were planned.

When Roger was 11 years old, his foster family of seven years suddenly decided to move to a southern state and to leave Roger behind. The Huntoons gave Roger's biracial heritage as their reason, but the escalation of difficulties between them and the child was considered a more fundamental motive for the abandonment. They announced the wish to sever all ties—no telephone calls, letters, or visits.

In this traumatic context CPS placed Roger in a new home, that of a single white woman, Ms. Fried, and her biracial 14-year-old adopted son. She had been waiting to adopt another biracial child.

Roger's difficulties in this new placement included an antagonistic denial of his black heritage and complaints about Ms. Fried's cooking. Mealtimes became so tense that his foster mother preferred to eat alone. Roger did, however, establish a good relationship with his foster brother. At the urging of Ms. Fried, the CPS worker arranged for Roger to receive evaluation and treatment at the same child guidance clinic where he previously had been in treatment. Her resistance to mental health assistance resulted in only tenuous cooperation with the clinic, but after twenty-nine sessions Roger showed much improvement. His adjustment to a new school also was satisfactory, and his peer relationships improved. The therapist's comments are summarized as follows:

> Roger is a friendly, likeable boy with a long history of rejection and loss. His failure to thrive in his first foster home was a particularly powerful organizing influence in Roger's early life. Now after years of nurturance and growth with the Huntoons he has been extruded again. This has been a major loss for Roger, generating tremendous anger and a terrible blow to his sense of worth.
>
> This is complicated even further by Roger's recent involvement with his biological parents, both of them schizophrenic, one of them black and the other white. One of his difficulties with the Huntoons was probably directly related to the long-kept secret about his parents. Just as he was trying to deal with his fantasies of rejection at birth by these parents, Roger was then rejected in reality by his long-term foster family.
>
> On being able to verbalize the sadness at that loss, Roger began to identify himself as black. His appearance, musical tastes, heroes, and interests all became very decidedly black.

As Ms. Fried's plans to adopt became solidified, Roger's biological mother was approached about giving up her parental rights. Roger himself talked to his mother, telling her of his wish to be adopted. Soon after this meeting, the mother had a psychotic relapse and again was hospitalized. Ms. Fried, who seemed eager to adopt Roger, was upset about the possibility of a delay.

In the ensuing months, Roger was involved in several serious incidents, including spray painting a neighbor's car, "accidentally" stabbing a boy's hand, setting fire to newspapers instead of delivering them, and running away for a short time. Roger evidently showed no remorse, nor did he attempt to deny these actions. He claimed that his suicidal attempt to run under a truck had been a mistake. During this time his performance at school—now junior high—suffered, as did his personal hygiene.

By the time Roger was arrested for shoplifting, Ms. Fried had become disheartened by Roger's rejection of her family, and she experienced growing doubts about her wish to adopt him. Urged by the CPS worker and a clinical consultant who recognized Roger's extreme need for help, Ms. Fried agreed to his admission to a hospital ward for psychiatrically disturbed children 21 months after he had come to live with her.

Roger, then almost 13, stayed on the psychiatric ward for two and one half months. Despite an initial difficulty with food, Roger adapted well to the program, began to form friendships, and clearly demonstrated his potential for leadership and the capacity for working through feelings about himself and his past.

As the discharge date approached, Ms. Fried, who had participated in the program, and Roger himself both showed reluctance about his return to Ms. Fried's household. After a period of uncertainty, the hospital staff in conjunction with the CPS worker recommended that yet another home be found. A black couple with grown children, Mr. and Mrs. Caldwell, seemed eager to welcome Roger on a long-term basis, with the possibility of adoption.

In his discharge summary, the child psychologist wrote: "Roger is a boy who has suffered because of inappropriate and harmful placements since birth. This has produced large amounts of stress on this genetically vulnerable child. He has developed defenses of denial and repression to deal, often adaptively, with the major losses in his life. It is understandable that he is hesitant to commit himself emotionally. But there are still indications that he desires the support of a family."

Considerations in this case:

1. Sustained continuity of adequate care is essential for all children, especially those who have been deprived or repeatedly placed with long-term or adoptive parents who reject them. Ironically, these rejections may themselves be a response to the provocative recovery behavior often associated with overcoming previous rejections and deprivations. In such cases, infusions of optimism from families or agencies, despite overwhelming disruptions, may help to "win the day."

2. Mixed racial origins complicate placement, but the principles remain the same.

3. The ultimate result of the CPS worker's unflagging efforts on behalf of the child dramatically demonstrates the value of a persistent, continuing effort by the agency and the worker. In fact, this worker provided leadership and inspiration for the various collaborating agencies and foster families involved.

Follow-up:

The CPS worker, on a recent visit, reported that after one year with the Caldwells Roger seemed to be doing fine and looked forward to his adoption, which was expected soon. Mr. and Mrs. Caldwell were in a food business, which Roger enjoyed. He offered the worker something to eat, which he himself pronounced delicious, but with the disclaimer, "You may not like it. It's soul food." The worker believed that Roger had found himself through these parents, who were both loving and strict, and that the ten weeks he spent on a children's psychiatric ward represented an important turning point in his life.

Visitation Conflicts

A child's best interests may be subverted when visitation is imposed on the basis of consideration for or fairness to the adults involved.

CASE 28

Randolph. The deleterious effects of forced and prolonged visitation.

The story of Randolph Collier illustrates a situation in which enforced visitation jeopardized the well-being (and perhaps the placement) of an 8-year-old boy.

Randolph spent his first year with his battling parents. At the age of 4 months, he was referred to CPS as uncared for and at risk of injury. The many services offered to the family were to no avail. When Mr. and Mrs. Collier were arrested for assaulting one another and Mrs. Collier was hospitalized, Randolph, then 14 months old, was committed to CPS and placed in a foster home. This placement ended when Mr. Collier threatened the foster mother; she in turn requested Randolph's removal.

Randolph, then 1½, again was placed, this time more successfully, and he remained with the new family for almost four years. During this interlude his parents were divorced and his father remarried. Visitation with his father continued on weekends, with Randolph's return to him as the goal. Randolph's mother was not available as a caretaker. The return took place soon before the child's fifth birthday and ushered in a very difficult time for him.*

Randolph, who slept on a downstairs sofa and had no toys, was abused both verbally and physically by his father and stepmother, who also physically assaulted one another. When his bruises and scratches began to arouse the suspicions of school authorities and others, Randolph divulged to the CPS worker that he was being abused. He was removed—after an eight-month stay—and placed in foster care with the Grants, Randolph's paternal aunt and her husband.

The following year, when Randolph was 6 years of age, a court-ordered evaluation revealed him to be:

---

*In retrospect, the child's best interests—or the least detrimental alternative for him—would have been better served had he been able to remain permanently with his long-term foster parents.

a handsome boy of "average" ability, currently impeded by emotional difficulties and low self-esteem. . . . Considering his life history, such feelings are unfortunately understandable. Randolph sees his parents as frightening and dangerous. He does not wish further visitation with them. He is reluctant to deal with his father at all. He is angry at him and fearful of being harmed by him. He sees his foster family as loving and safe. . . . Yet, because of the limbo he is in, he does not yet feel a part of them.

The psychologist also reported that the Grants wished to adopt Randolph. After his year with them, Randolph had improved in emotional outlook, behavior, and hygiene and now took pride in his appearance. Mr. Grant, a carpenter, gave him a great deal of individual attention, taking him on work calls and other trips. Mrs. Grant, however, expressed much concern about Randolph's continuing contact with his biological parents. She believed that visits with them caused Randolph to regress in his behavior. He began to lie, wet his bed, and have nightmares. A psychologist recommended that Randolph be freed for adoption, preferably by the Grants, and that he receive therapy. He stated, "The legal limbo of foster placement with visitation with his parents is *not* in his best interests."

Despite this recommendation, visitation with both biological parents and their spouses (Randolph's mother had married again), which had been reduced and then temporarily suspended, was resumed by court order the following year when Randolph was 7. As documented by his therapist's letters to CPS, his behavior increasingly deteriorated. The therapist noted that Randolph's anxiety now was affecting every facet of his life. His hyperactivity in school impeded his learning. In therapy he was becoming increasingly withdrawn and unreachable, and at home his destructive behavior—soiling, lying, having tantrums—became intolerable. The CPS worker learned from discussions with the therapist that there was a direct relation between Randolph's dreaded visits and his loss of control. She recommended, to no avail, that the visits be suspended.

A year later, the CPS worker requested a reassessment of Randolph's visitation order, which was carried out by the same psychologist. His report reaffirmed that Randolph's psychological parents were the Grants. "It is *strongly* recommended that visitation with his biological parents be ended immediately. A therapeutic goodbye session with each may be advisable at some point, under strict supervision by Randolph's therapist and CPS worker. This is necessary for his psychological survival. It is further strongly recommended, as it was last year, that there be *immediate termination of parental rights.*"

The aunt and uncle also opposed visitation with the parents but preferred to remain permanent foster parents rather than adopt Randolph because of their stated concern for the biological father's physical health, which had deteriorated in the past year. The aunt feared that a termination or adoption proceeding might "kill" her brother. A consultation with another child expert reinforced the notion that Randolph should remain with his long-term foster parents, his aunt and uncle. Since the aunt and uncle did not wish to adopt and the court was reluctant to grant termination without an adoption plan in place, the petition for the termination of parental rights was withdrawn. The consultant further underscored the recommendation that visits with the biological parents not be resumed. The court suspended the parents' visitation rights.

Considerations in this case:

1. The decision making was complicated both desirably and undesirably by the use of relatives as potential adoptive/foster parents. The desirable complication is the creation of the rich continuity of the extended family. The undesirable complication is that any conflict or ambivalence in the relationship between the adoptive/foster and biological parents is much more difficult to resolve or contain when kinship is involved.

2. In such a case, it is difficult to know which has been more deleterious—the abuse, the abandonment, the multiple placements, or the forced visitation. The combination is overwhelming.

Follow-up:
In his twelfth year, Randolph's difficulties mounted. He was hospitalized because of his impaired ability to function socially and academically. The cumulative effect of the trauma and deprivation in earlier childhood seemed to be devastating. The uncertainty of his future was suggested in the plan to move him to a long-term residential treatment center.

CASE 29
Edward. A child as pawn in a ten-year struggle between biological parents, foster parents, CPS, and the courts.

When Edward Pascale was 2 weeks old, he was physically abused by his mother, who at the time was experiencing a postpartum psychosis. He suffered many bruises and abrasions, fractures of two ribs and a clavicle, and weight loss. His parents initially claimed that he had refused to eat and that his injuries were caused by his 1-year-old sister. During Edward's hospitalization, a psychiatrist evaluated Mr. and Mrs. Pascale, who were noted to have severe marital problems.

Following "voluntary" placement by CPS, Edward spent three and a half months in one foster home and five months in another. Antagonism between Mrs. Pascale and the two successive foster mothers concerning visitation appeared to be responsible for these moves. At 8 months Edward was placed with a third foster family, the Jorgensens, with whom he still lives.

Although he had adapted slowly to his first two placements, Edward's adjustment to the Jorgensen family took even longer. Blandness of affect, resistance to cuddling, and episodes of panicky screaming at bedtime were signs of his distress.

At the age of 17 months Edward was evaluated by a child development expert, who found him to be about six months delayed, especially in the areas of language and social relationships. The psychiatrist was also struck by the biological mother's "severe abnormality in parenting." He recommended that parental rights be terminated as soon as possible and visitation discontinued immediately, stressing that Edward was a very vulnerable child with special needs. Despite expert recommendations and efforts by CPS, the court denied the petition to terminate parental rights but also refused the parents' petition for revocation of the state's custody. Edward was kept in limbo.

Visits with his biological mother had been difficult for Edward from the outset, and he reacted to them symptomatically. During his first two years, for example, his behavior would become disorganized after a visit. He often had a stiff neck, excessive regurgitation, diarrhea, and screaming spells. Mrs. Jorgensen, the continuing foster parent, believed the child was terrified by the required visits.

Under Mrs. Jorgensen's care, which included attendance in a preschool program, by age 3 Edward showed increased socialization, greater cognitive capacity, and more consistent behavior. Later that year, a new CPS worker filed a second petition for termination of parental rights. The judge declined to hear the suit, but instead ordered a new psychiatric evaluation, recommending that CPS "make determined effort to assist in the reintegration of the family." This court-ordered impasse required that Edward visit with his biological parents and prevented his foster family from adopting him, as they wished to do. The coercive visits led to Edward's protests against visiting, anger toward his foster parents, depression and fearfulness, clinging behavior, and extreme fatigue.

When he was almost 6 years old, Edward was referred to an emergency psychiatric service, with fire setting as the presenting behavioral symptom and some suicidal ideation. Short-term treatment alleviated his symptoms but at the time no long-term assistance was accessible. The following year Edward suffered from anxiety and stress caused by the precariousness of his placement. He underwent yet another evaluation. As a result, he was enrolled in a learning disabilities program, and treatment was initiated.

When Edward was 8 years old, his therapist, commenting on his "fragmented sense of reality," observed: "Ed has such a poor sense of self . . . that he often represents himself as an inanimate object. . . . The trauma of multiple legal proceedings and placements has severely affected Eddie's emotional and academic development, as he continues to be a pawn in the seven year struggle between his natural parents, his foster parents, and CPS. A custody decision, whatever the outcome, is vital to Ed's development."

Later that year, a judge at last agreed with CPS that weekly visitation should be terminated. The child psychiatrist soon after observed "an unequivocal clinical improvement. Edward is noticeably calmer at home and in the treatment sessions." Unfortunately, within several months Edward's biological mother, violating the judge's order, began to accost him in his neighborhood and in the schoolyard with such remarks as "I'm your real mommy, you were in my tummy, you belong to me." These contacts, reported to CPS by the distraught foster mother, exacerbated Edward's behavioral symptoms. When Edward was 9½, the therapist wrote:

> For Ed, the fear of loss of a consistent person or parent figure(s) is so great that he takes on a chameleon-like attitude. His alliances switch when he jockeys back and forth between the two different parental homes, and in this psychological ping-pong Ed loses any real focus on how he feels. . . . It is clear that the overriding issue is conclusion of the interminable legal proceedings in the context of abundant clinical evidence in support of termination of parental rights.

And again, soon before his tenth birthday, "The major ongoing stressor for Ed is chronic non-resolution of custody litigation. . . . The trial has just ended; the decision is pending."

Considerations in this case:

1. This case illustrates the psychological devastation suffered by a child whose need for permanency and consistency was denied by the legal system. The situation was kept at the level of a boiling, destructive conflict by the contending adults.

2. This child was caught for ten years in a forced, frightening visitation with his abusive biological parents. These corrosive visits were demonstrably harmful to this vulnerable child and continued in the context of a stalemate between CPS and the courts.

3. Repeated recommendations by child experts for termination of parental rights, buttressing the CPS petitions, were to no avail.

4. The child's opportunity for adoption by a nurturing family who wanted him and with whom he had lived for nine years continued to be denied.

Follow-up:

A termination petition finally was granted and upheld on appeal. Edward was adopted in his eleventh year, having been in foster care since the age of 2 weeks and with his adoptive family from the age of 8 months.

Other Placement Issues

Talking to Children

Once a decision to remove a child from home has been made, the Guidelines make it explicit that "a social service plan of action between *DCYS and the parent* must be developed to explain why the child has been removed."* This plan is put in writing to ensure that the parents and the social worker have an agreement, as well as an evaluative basis for continuing or changing it. It is also im-

*See appendix 1.

portant for the worker to communicate directly with the child the reasons for his or her removal and the plan for the future.

Workers should acquire the skill of talking to children. This enables them to explain to children why they are being moved, where they will live, and who will take care of them and to assure them that their new "parents" will provide them with food, shelter, and loving care. A worker's skill is based on a combination of intuition, training, and experience. The conversation between child and worker is a crucial first step toward preparing a child to benefit from her or his move into a new family. The worker describes the placement and also empathizes with the child's inevitable feelings of abandonment, helplessness, and anger, as well as apprehensions about a threatening unknown. Children awaiting placement benefit if they are able to review the past as a preparation for the future. They may experience resentment and fear about what has happened to the parents from whom they are being separated. During these discussions, the worker promises to be available to the child by saying, for example, "I'll be coming to see you next Wednesday at 4:00 P.M., unless I call, and I'll ask your new father or mother to show you where this is on the calendar." It is also useful if the worker calls the new parent to ask how "things are going." The children's age and development are, of course, crucial factors in determining how to talk to them.

CASE 30

Lily, Trent, and Susie. Children belatedly told the reasons for their removal from the home.

In this case a worker talked to two young children, Trent, age 4, and Lily, 6, about sexual abuse and explained why their placement was necessary. Trent had confided to his maternal grandmother that his father had repeatedly molested him sexually. That same week Mr. Baldwin admitted this to a counselor with whom he had been working for some time. Mr. Baldwin was arrested and awaited trial on criminal charges. The children were removed from the home. Unfortunately, the maternal grandmother could not take care of all three children. Lily and her baby sister, Susie, were placed with a CPS foster family, and Trent with his maternal grandparents. Both father and mother agreed that the children should not be with them at this time.

Several months later it became evident to a new CPS worker that the children did not understand why they no longer were living at home. No one had discussed the subject with them, neither the former CPS worker nor either set of parents, biological or foster. After Trent's disclosure, his grandmother read a book to him about "good touches" and "bad touches," but no further explanation was given.

The new worker attempted to clarify the issue individually with the two older children. Lily denied having had any thoughts about her removal from her parents or any knowledge of the book her grandmother had read to Trent. The worker explained to Lily that some grownups have a problem and play with children's private parts. "We had to take you children from home because your Daddy was playing with Trent's penis in that way."

Lily made no response. The worker continued, saying that Trent had been very brave to tell Grandma what had happened. "Grandma told us because she wanted us to help you and make sure that you're all right." Lily still remained silent, but the worker added, since "Daddy has this problem, you children need to be away from the home in order to be safe." It would have been more logical and better for the children if the father had moved out. However, as so often happens, the mother refused to bring charges, and the children's best interests were sacrificed to the parents' preference to stay together.

Although Lily had expressed little, the worker felt that she seemed to understand a good deal of what had been said. The worker accordingly told Lily that it was good to be able to talk about how you are feeling or what you are wondering about, and that she would be available to answer any questions Lily had. The worker also said that it would be all right to talk with her foster mother.

The worker was, of course, also much concerned about Trent, the abused 4-year-old boy. She spent time with him as well to clarify the reasons for his staying with his grandparents. Trent, like his sister, did not respond directly, but talked about other problems at home, such as fighting and hitting. The worker reported, "We talked about what happened last summer, about the story Grandma had read to him and how upset it made him feel. He remembered. I told him how good it was that he told Grandma what had been happening to him—what Daddy had done. Even a Daddy shouldn't do that. It was good that Grandma called me for help."

Trent at one point said that he wanted to live at home with his parents. The worker responded that she, too, hoped he would be back with his parents some day, but that he was safer now with his grandparents. Trent was seen in consultation at the CPS Crisis Intervention Center and referred for ongoing therapy. The worker noted, "It is felt that we have not yet seen the full impact of what Trent has experienced." The worker also arranged for visits between Trent and his sisters and some carefully regulated visits of the children with their parents in the CPS office. She was alert to how the children were adjusting to their new homes, which overall proved to be satisfactory.

Considerations in this case:

1. The sexual abuse of a 4-year-old boy by his father led to the removal of three children from their home, rather than to the removal of the father.

2. Because of the charged subject of sexual abuse, the children were given little, if any, explanation about their removal from their parents until several months later. The explanation was omitted because the first worker felt unable to discuss sexual matters with the children.

3. A new CPS worker gently explored with the older children

the reasons for their placement away from home, tailoring her remarks to their ages, experience, and capacity for understanding.

Follow-up:
Lily and Susie were subsequently adopted by the foster family with whom they originally had been placed. Trent was adopted by friends of his sisters' new family who lived in a neighboring state.

Sibling Placement
More than half of all children placed in adoptive or foster homes have siblings (Ward 1984, 321). As Goldstein, Freud, and Solnit (1979) state:

> Children raised together have a common background and experience that usually is characterized by companionship, rivalry, and mutual support in times of common threat or need. Staying together enables children to support each other by buffering the traumatic family breakup. It provides children with a sense of ongoing community, the continuity that strengthens them in coping with felt threats to future security and self-esteem, and with guilt feelings and associated defensive reactions (p. 32).

The importance of the sibling tie requires assessment and understanding by the worker in order to construct a plan that will be responsive to the child's needs. These include intimacy, safety and comfort, and continuity in relationships with brothers and sisters at a time when the children's tie to a caretaker is being traumatically threatened or ruptured, even if temporarily. If separation is required because the state lacks emergency placement for a group of siblings, the reunification of the children should be assured as soon as possible.

Rationalizations frequently used for separating siblings are that a home for several children is unavailable; that separating siblings will be good for them because their needs are too great for one parent to handle; that children with special needs require the undivided attention of parents; that the solution to intense sibling rivalry is to separate the children; and that maintaining siblings together will unrealistically encourage the children to expect the reunification of the family.

The presumption should be that siblings always be placed together, unless careful individual assessment of each child and of the relationship between the children reveals that the tie either is not significant or is superseded by other factors, such as age, disparate developmental levels, or the length of previous separations. In addition, the harsh reality is that a suitable home for several siblings is not always available. The following case exemplifies this situation.

CASE 31

The Davis children. Placement of siblings, together or not?

When many children in the same family require placement, such as happened with the Davises, a worker may feel overwhelmed. The Guidelines state, "Children should be removed . . . if they are not wanted." In this case, six siblings gradually were abandoned over a four-year period by their drug-addicted mother, whose actions, despite her protestations, clearly showed that she did not want them.

Mrs. Davis requested temporary foster home placement for her five children, Martin, 12, Ralph, 10, Elmer, 9, Michelle, 5, and Graham, 4. Her husband, the children's father, had no interest in their care. A CPS social worker helped this mother enter a drug rehabilitation program and placed the children in several homes, hoping that they could remain in touch with their mother. Within a few months, Mrs. Davis dropped out of the program and disappeared. The following winter the children, who in the meantime had had only sporadic contact with their mother, were committed to CPS. The next spring Mrs. Davis revived her contact with CPS and reentered the rehabilitation program. Later that year, soon after the death of her husband, she gave birth to Cassie, her sixth child.

Approximately one year after the children had been placed, Mrs. Davis completed the rehabilitation program with apparent success and was reunited with her children, much to their joy. For a while all seemed to go well. Unfortunately, after several months she again requested that the children be temporarily placed. At this time Cassie also was committed to CPS. Mrs. Davis did not fulfill the terms of agreement in a short-term contract. She resumed the use of drugs and again vanished. She had intermittent contact with her sons during this period, but contrary to her promises, for six months she failed to stay in touch with her daughters.

The situation of these six children—then in three separate placements—presented the CPS worker with a very difficult problem, which was compounded not only by the children's feelings of loyalty toward and love for their mother, but also by their unusually strong ties to one another. The worker described them all as "very nice people," whose poignant memories of their former family life and wistful dreams of its return mitigated against the formation of new attachments. The older children especially continued to be protective of Mrs. Davis, despite her broken promises to them. They expressed concern and anxiety about the well-being of their younger siblings, who they believed badly needed their mother.

At this juncture the CPS worker felt overwhelmed. Her own hopes for Mrs. Davis's rehabilitation also had been raised repeatedly, and she inevitably shared the children's feelings of loss, disappointment, anger, and grief. Furthermore, she had to deal with the formidable task of finding arrangements that would be acceptable to these children and would provide the best opportunity for new attachments to take root. The problem was presented to a clinical consultant and resulted in the following recommendations: to look at each child individually, taking into account each one's age, developmental capacities, and relationship to their mother and siblings; to consider the alternative placements which would be available to each; and to include all the children in the discussion and planning process.

The worker followed through on this plan with skill and sensitivity. Over a period of six months, and four years after the initial placement, she ingeniously arranged several meetings in a nearby park with all the children present, in which various possibilities for each one were considered and weighed. She also met individually more than once with each child to assess his or her personality, developmental needs, and plans for placement.

The Davis children were at this time, respectively, aged 16, 14, 13, 9, 8, and 1. According to the worker's assessments, Martin, the oldest child, most identified with his mother. He urged that she be given another chance, blamed the state for her troubles, and had the greatest influence with the other children. Martin had not done well in his foster home and was having trouble in school. He could not tolerate the intensity of relationships in a family. The best plan for him, given his adolescence, seemed to be living in a group home, which might provide less intense individual living arrangements than those of regular family life. He was encouraged to actively seek contact with his mother and also to keep in touch with his siblings.

Ralph and Elmer, ages 14 and 13, were helped by the worker to understand and work through their feelings about their mother. They were able to speak of their sadness at her inability to look after them and at her rejection of them. It was decided that they would continue to live in the foster home on a permanent basis but not be adopted. They wished to keep their names and the tie to their biological family.

Michelle, age 9, originally had been placed in a foster home that did not work out. She was placed again at age 8 in another home, where she was adopted. Although she missed her mother, she also was aware of having been abandoned, especially as Mrs. Davis had made no contact after the second placement. Michelle responded favorably to the idea of adoption—as she put it, "staying there forever"—and also of having her baby sister, Cassie, with her. She wanted her mother to know where she was and to visit her.

Graham, age 8, had not gotten along in his foster home and had been very unhappy. His maternal aunt, who had wished to help but could not take in all six of the children, agreed to take Graham. She became his legal guardian, the guardianship having been transferred to her via the Juvenile Court.

Cassie, 12 months old, was placed in the same adoptive home as her sister, Michelle.

The story of the Davis children exemplifies a creative solution to a difficult problem. The CPS worker provided these children with continuity and with the opportunity for another start in life. Rather than succumb to anger, frustration, or helplessness in re-action to the behavior of a drug-addicted mother, the worker con-sidered each child as a person in his or her own right. Since it was not possible for the children, mutually attached as they were, to be together, the worker proceeded to find the next best course of action. Arrangements were made so that each of the five younger children could be with one other member of his or her biological family: the second and third boys together in their foster family, the two girls together in their adoptive family, and the youngest boy with his maternal aunt as legal guardian.

The worker's expertise and her investment of time and caring were impressive. Seven years after the case first came to the at-tention of CPS, the outcome was more favorable than could have been anticipated. The children continued to have contact with their mother to the extent of her ability, were in touch with each other, and apparently were adjusting well to their new lives. A crucial element was the worker's understanding of the personalities of these spirited children and her respect for their needs. She helped to support their sense of continuity. Encouragement of their participation in the planning process both for their own and one another's lives enabled these young people to maintain such family integrity and cohesion as was feasible. The worker and her consultant were able to determine what was least harmful for each of the children and for the group as a whole.

Considerations in this case:

1. The worker, at first overwhelmed by the task of planning for six children abandoned by a drug-addicted mother, confronted two problems of placement: Would the children's ties and loyalty to their mother interfere with the formation of new relationships? What arrangements could be made that would respect their unusually strong sibling ties and their protectiveness of one another?

2. It would have been preferable to keep the children together to retain their ties to one another and their sense of community.

3. Since no single home was available, the five younger children were placed in homes that enabled them to remain in touch with each other, two sets in pairs and the fifth with a relative. The worker included all the children in the planning and discussion of their future.

Follow-up:

Three years later, Martin, age 19, had successfully completed his training in the Job Corps. He had recently stopped by to see the worker and to tell her of his employment. He felt good about himself. Ralph and Elmer, ages 17 and 16, were getting along satisfactorily. Mrs. Davis had recently visited them for a week in their foster home, and they had also visited with other relatives. Michelle, age 12, was reported to be doing well, although the worker believed that she eventually might need to work out her conflicted feelings about her mother. Graham, age 11, was said to be doing well, although he had had some difficulty several months before and was referred for counseling by the worker. Ralph and Elmer reported that when they had last seen him he was doing fine. A developmental examination of Cassie, age 4, indicated good progress.

Children and AIDS

CASE 32

Fiona and her sisters. A mother with AIDS and the case management of her children.

Shortly before the birth of her third daughter, Fiona, Ms. Turin was diagnosed as having AIDS. She was being treated in the drug and alcohol unit in the hospital where Fiona was born. Several weeks premature, Fiona weighed four pounds, eight ounces at birth and tested HIV positive. She suffered from symptoms of heroin and cocaine withdrawal and spent her first three months in the hospital's neonatal intensive care unit. The hospital referred the case to CPS because of concern about Ms. Turin's ability to provide a stable living situation for the child.

Fiona was discharged from the hospital under CPS supervision to the care of a maternal aunt, in whose home her mother and half-sisters were living. Soon after, the mother was incarcerated for larceny and criminal trespass charges. Because the aunt did not wish to keep her, Fiona, then 3 months old, was placed in foster care. Her foster mother, Ms. Redmond, was a 46-year-old single woman and an experienced nurse who provided care for children diagnosed with life-threatening diseases, primarily AIDS.

Because of Fiona's HIV status, she received ongoing medical care at a pediatric immunology clinic every three months. For the next two years, repeated HIV tests found her to be free of the AIDS virus. At the present state of knowledge, it is presumed that she is free of AIDS.

At the time of Fiona's placement, Teresa and Willa, her half-sisters, were also removed from their aunt's home and placed in another specially licensed home with a friend of their mother, where they remained for two years. This was a particularly traumatic time for Willa. Willa had a stormy relationship with her mother and often called attention to herself by self-destructive behavior.

When the girls were 1, 4, and 6 years old, they were legally

committed to CPS with their mother's consent for an eighteen-
month planning period. CPS extended this commitment for
another eighteen months. During this period, Ms. Turin was incarcerated twice for shoplifting. Upon her first release, she visited
her children frequently but often arrived drunk or high. She was
also beginning to experience the first of many AIDS-related ill-
nesses. Ms. Turin's fourth arrest, for shoplifting and assaulting an
employee, resulted in a six-month prison sentence.

While in prison, Ms. Turin used health care services and counseling productively and received regular visits from her children.
The components of the commitment agreement included a pro-
jected reunification plan contingent on Ms. Turin's continued use
of medical care, involvement in a drug and alcohol treatment program, acceptance of supervised child management, and location
of an apartment.

Released from prison and awarded custody of her three children, Ms. Turin at first stayed with her sister, but the increasing
deterioration of her health made reunification unrealistic. A year
later, in order to be with Fiona as much as possible, Ms. Turin
moved in with Ms. Redmond, Fiona's continuing foster mother.
Within two months, Ms. Turin's physical condition had greatly
worsened, and, at the time of an emergency hospitalization, her
death seemed imminent.

In the presence of a lawyer, Ms. Turin voluntarily relinquished
her parental rights and expressed the wish that Ms. Redmond
adopt all three of her daughters. The older girls, having visited her
often, felt close ties to Ms. Redmond and their half-sister. Furthermore, they were soon to have another placement because their foster mother was planning to leave the country. Psychological evaluations had revealed that Teresa and, especially, Willa were in
much need of stability, consistency, and affection.

Ms. Redmond expressed interest in adopting all three children.
This plan was endorsed by CPS, with the further recommendation that the parental rights of the three fathers be terminated.

None of the fathers had shown even minimal interest in the children.

Ms. Turin's physical condition improved in some respects, but at the same time, according to her physicians, she began to show behavioral symptoms of AIDS dementia. She moved out of Ms. Redmond's home, claiming to have been "tricked" into terminating her parental rights and insisting unrealistically that she wished either to care for her children herself or to place them with her mother in another state. However, she did not even know her mother's whereabouts.

Ms. Turin's suspiciousness in time focused on Ms. Redmond. Ms. Turin went to Ms. Redmond's home, where she accused Ms. Redmond of "stealing" her children and physically assaulted her. Ms. Turin was arrested and restrained by a court order from returning to the house. She subsequently claimed that she had believed Ms. Redmond to be the devil, who was attempting to poison her.

Following her attack on Ms. Redmond, Ms. Turin was referred for psychiatric help and forbidden by a court order to contact Ms. Redmond. The foster mother refused to permit visitation in her home but was ready, for the benefit of the children, to accommodate their supervised visits elsewhere with their mother.

Ms. Redmond's adoption of Fiona, whom she had "skillfully nurtured and lovingly cared for," was imminent. The social worker from the child guidance clinic strongly recommended that CPS facilitate her adoption of the two older girls as well. Teresa and Willa expressed concern for their mother but did not believe that she could take care of them. They looked forward to being part of Ms. Redmond's family.

Considerations in this case:

1. AIDS in pregnant women, especially when associated with multiple hard drug dependency, raises serious questions about the ability of these mothers to care for their children.

2. The transmission of AIDS from mothers to their infants is a threatening and possibly fatal situation for newborn children.

3. Children born to mothers who have AIDS face the uncertainty of how long their mothers will live and the certainty that they will die relatively soon. Thus, planning for such children is complex, requiring a tolerance for uncertainty and a case-by-case determination in order to apply the principles associated with best interests of children. For example, should continuity of affectionate relationships be modified in order to factor in the risk of both the physical and psychological challenges of AIDS?

Exit Process and Dynamics

An important and perhaps insufficiently recognized aspect of the CPS worker's task is the exit interview. This meeting with the committed child when he or she reaches age 18 marks the official end of the child welfare agency's responsibility. The purpose of the meeting is to review the circumstances under which the child came into agency care, the child's development as recorded by the agency, and a plan for the future. The interview also gives the young adult an opportunity to ask questions and learn more about his or her earlier life.

CASE 33

Donald. The benefits of an exit interview.

Donald Norwich, whose parents voluntarily terminated their rights when he was 7 months old, had been in foster care since the age of 3 months. He had always lived with the same family but was not adopted by them. Although the foster parents had divorced several years before, Donald continued to make his permanent home with his foster mother and stayed in touch with his foster father as well.

During his CPS exit interview, Donald's worker of several years gave him his birth certificate and information about his biological parents. Donald learned that his unmarried mother had given birth to a son five years before he was born. Since Donald's father offered no financial support, his mother felt that she could not care for another child. The worker told Donald his mother's birthplace and what was known of his father from the court study.

Donald and the worker together read through his case record. The worker was impressed with the intensity of Donald's interest in his own history and development: his weight at birth, first foods, first teeth, toilet training, and descriptions of him at various stages. "An attractive child whose responsive, animated face gives him a very pleasing, happy personality." "A most adorable 10 month old child who crawls backward and is attempting to walk." "A very appealing 2½ year old with curly hair and medium colored skin. He speaks in sentences and very distinctly."

As the worker read through the case record, Donald took notes and wanted to hear all of it, "all the little things," which they discussed: his grades, his trumpet and clarinet lessons and love of music, his enthusiasm for basketball and soccer in the eleventh grade, which had replaced an earlier lack of interest in sports.

The enjoyment shared by Donald and the worker was impressive. The meeting was genuinely satisfying.

Considerations in this case:

1. The exit interview presented an opportunity for the CPS worker to review the reasons for the child's placement at 3 months. It provided concrete facts about his background and development, helped him to gain a realistic sense of his self-worth, and to have more confidence in his own identity.

2. A long-standing relationship between the CPS worker and the client created an atmosphere of trust, in which the young man, better able to understand his own history, could begin to plan for his future.

3. As a result of such an interview, should the individual wish to contact his biological parent(s), the worker would offer to help explore this wish. If the parent(s) were unwilling, the worker would be in a position to provide support to the disappointed youth.

4. The issues of identity and self-esteem are paramount, and the availability of a sensitive worker is invaluable in providing support.

A different kind of exit interview is described below. A middle-aged man, by investigating his past, not only solved its mystery but also found himself to be more fulfilled as a person.

CASE 34

David Nelson Natwick. An adoptee's gratifying search.

A successful civil engineer, who had been adopted as an infant, began a quest at the age of 50 for his biological parents. He contacted the child guidance clinic that had been involved in his pre-adoption screening process. A staff social worker located his chart, and the following story unfolded.

David Nelson Natwick's initial letter to the clinic reported "an inner desire to learn of my origin" and also made clear the strength of his psychological ties with his adoptive family, who had given him "a wonderful fifty years. . . . I wouldn't have wanted it any other way."

David's adoptive mother and father, a minister in a small town, already had one son; a second son had been stillborn five years later. Mr. and Mrs. Natwick, feeling a need to fill the void created by this loss, found David through an adoption agency. He lived with them from the age of 6 months. That first year, following the requirements of the time, the course of his development was examined periodically by experts at the clinic. The Natwicks officially adopted David when he was 2, and they subsequently had a daughter and another son.

When David was 6 or 7 years old, Mrs. Natwick told him that she and her husband were not his biological parents but that they loved him as much as their other children and that he always would be just as important to them. In an autobiographical sketch, David wrote of his adoptive mother, "She was a wonderful person and a very stabilizing force in my life, who shaped my life and my de-

velopment more than any other person. She had tremendous fore-
sight and understanding, and always seemed to be able to deal with
my down times with calmness and confidence. She was an extremely reassuring person."

When David was 13, Mrs. Natwick told him the important fact
that his name, David Nelson, had been given him at birth and
retained by the Natwicks, who had completed it with their own
surname. This information surprised and pleased the child, and
he wrote much later: "It is a special part of my heritage and the
only thing I have that was given to me by my natural mother."
Mrs. Natwick also told David that she possessed many letters concerning his adoption, which he was free to read whenever he
wished to do so. Of this he wrote, "I really *did* want to see them
but was afraid to ask for them for fear that it would upset my
folks." For this reason, and perhaps for other reasons of his own,
David waited some thirty-seven years before pursuing this matter
further.

The Natwick family moved to the West Coast when David was
5. He did well both at home and in school, made friends, and
developed skills and hobbies. After three years in the navy, he went
to college, where he majored in engineering. While there, he met
and married his wife. He had been in his present job for more than
twenty years. Unable to have children of their own, David and his
wife adopted a daughter and, two years later, a son. Both were
now teenagers and flourishing.

Coming east in pursuit of his quest, David began to discover
his "roots" through the help of the social worker at the child guidance clinic and records provided by the adoption agency. He
learned that he had been born out of wedlock to a 17-year-old
mother and a 51-year-old father. His first contacts were with his
stepsisters, the children of his father's third wife, who welcomed
him warmly. He saw photographs of both biological parents and
movies of his now dead father, for whom he felt a particular affin-
ity. He wrote to the social worker:

Emotionally it was quite moving for me—I would have a difficult time describing my feelings except to say they were all very positive. I felt like a great shroud had been lifted and I was feeling good about my past for the first time. Always before it had been a great mystery and I didn't know whether to feel good or bad about it. It was always an unknown in my life and walking into it after 50 years, not knowing what I'd find, was rather scary.

David's main goal of meeting his biological mother proved more difficult. Having discovered her whereabouts, he proceeded to court her with sensitivity and kindness. He concluded an autobiographical sketch, "I wrote [this] because I wanted to share my experiences with a person who is special to me, whom I recently found, but whom I have yet to meet. That special person is my natural mother. To her I dedicate this story in hopes it will provide the catalyst which will eventually bring understanding and an opportunity to meet and share our thoughts."

Having mailed the sketch to his mother, David sent flowers to her on several occasions and also "low key" letters. He wrote the social worker, "I tried to make it clear that I do not wish to intrude in her life . . . but that I certainly would be receptive to a meeting if that was her choice." In one letter to his mother, David had told her of his temptation to telephone her, thereby giving her the option of changing her telephone to an unlisted number.

About a year later, encouraged by his mother's acceptance of all his communications (sent by registered mail) and retention of the same telephone number, David included a note with his flowers. The note informed her that he was nearby and planning to call her. They met at her house on the same day.

David later described this event as one that had "cleared the highest hurdle." He also discovered, after meeting her, that he had little in common with his mother. He learned that his father had been an executive and that his mother had for years worked as a housekeeper. A recent widow, she had had no other children. She had not acknowledged his many communications because she did not know what to say. She told David that his father had been "a bad man."

By this time, however, David had formed a highly positive view of his biological father, based for the most part on accounts of him by his devoted stepdaughters. Indeed, whereas David's actual meeting with his mother had been informative, it seemed incidental by comparison with the significance of his discovery of his biological father. As David wrote to the social worker, he had found that he and his father shared "many of the same traits, likes and characteristics. . . . It causes me to realize that some of the emotional feelings I . . . couldn't understand, were normal and inherited. It is a wonderful feeling to understand it all."

A sidelight of David's story is the reactions of other members of his adoptive family. This family, and especially his adoptive father, then 89 years old, always had been interested in and supportive of David's search. David described Mr. Natwick as "a great man [who] has always had a tremendous interest in me. He has always been 'in my corner,' supporting anything I undertake."

David's wife, however, was initially uncomfortable about the search. She feared that her own adopted children might wish to investigate their biological backgrounds and thereby jeopardize their relationship with her. The children seemed interested in the search but "rather noncommittal." David speculated that they might feel as he had at their age, afraid that any show of interest in their own past might upset their adoptive mother. He wrote:

> In *my case* I really believe my teenage life would have been less stressful had I known then what I know now. I am not advocating this approach for all adoption cases, but in my case—yes. My adoptive parents, Mom and Dad, were the greatest two parents a person could have. . . . They were very caring and giving people and I love them dearly. I

wouldn't have wanted my life to have been any other way. Becoming aware of my biological family has not changed my feelings about my adoptive family—they are still my family—my *number one* family!!

Considerations in this case:

1. The interest in knowing about one's origins and earlier development may arise in adolescence and not be acted on until middle age. The timing for discovery is best determined by the individual who is in search of himself or herself.

2. A 50-year-old adoptee, an intelligent and introspective man, gained from his search for his biological parents a sense of completeness and personal growth. He also gained a still greater appreciation of his adoptive and immediate family.

3. The data suggest that the strengths of the adoptive parents and those of their adopted son complemented each other and contributed to a mutual understanding and trust.

4. The inability of this man and his wife to have their own children probably activated and reinforced his dormant yearnings to discover his origins.

5. This case illustrates another kind of relationship between a client and a mental health worker. The worker had indispensable access to early records and provided continuous support, enabling the adoptee to recover and assimilate his past.

CASE 35
Mr. Pavan. "Who am I?"

A follow-up that can be viewed as a delayed exit interview, this case provides a snapshot of a 57-year-old man who was raised in the state's custody. Sometime after the death of his lifelong foster parents and a loss of contact with his brothers, Mr. Pavan, with his wife as his ally, had begun to wonder openly about his family origins.

In an initial meeting, the CPS worker learned that Mr. Pavan and his wife had some knowledge of his background. He had been told that a younger sibling had died under mysterious circumstances and that his mother had been incarcerated. He also knew that his brothers and uncles had been in the army.

The CPS worker enabled him to see the record. He discovered for the first time that his parents were not married and that his biological father was not Polish, as he had believed, but Italian.

During the next weeks, the Pavans continued their contact with the same CPS worker. Mrs. Pavan reported that her husband had shared his new information with their grown children but in private had said to her, "Who am I?" Mrs. Pavan, on her husband's behalf, later inquired whether his biological father had known of his son's existence. This question could not be answered, since the man's whereabouts were not known. The worker provided the wife with the names and addresses of her husband's relatives, with whom he planned to make contact.

About a month after the original meeting, the CPS worker called the Pavans to learn how they were assimilating this knowledge. Mrs. Pavan stated that her husband was accepting it well and recently had asked his neighbor, "How does it feel to have an Italian for a friend?"

Considerations in this case:

1. Following the death of his permanent foster parents, that is, his psychological parents, a man began the search for his biological parents. The question "Who am I?" quite likely had been preceded much earlier—if tacitly—by "Why did my parents give me up?" and "Why was I not adopted?"

2. Nevertheless, this foster child, now an adult, appeared to have many strengths. He had established an evidently happy marriage, with children. He was interested in pursuing questions about his heritage and able to assimilate the answers.

3. In this belated exit interview the social worker's skill and empathy enabled a former foster child to have more confidence about himself, past, present, and future.

6

Final

Perspectives

and

Conclusion

We have presented a range of cases that typify situations faced daily by CPS workers. Many cases illustrate how effective intervention and planning can lead to more favorable outcomes for the children involved. These cases are significant because they demonstrate that such interventions can make a critical difference in the lives of many children. On the other hand, some cases seem impossible. Solutions to them, however imperfect, necessitate the application of the principle of the least detrimental alternative. Such cases are significant in part because they indicate the limits of our knowledge. They also test our ability to make sensible exceptions, when indicated, to generally accepted principles. These cases often remind us as well of the resilience, capacity for adaptation, and unexpected potential of the human spirit.

Usually clients do not voluntarily seek CPS help. Workers therefore are confronted with the difficult job of providing assistance in a nonvoluntary setting. They must achieve a balance between the roles of helper and investigator. Strong support should be available to help them perform their tasks most effectively and deal with such disturbing feelings as helplessness, anger, and anxiety, which the demands of the work engender. Otherwise, frontline workers are at risk of experiencing themselves as isolated.

This book is based on principles of child development that we believe reflect the current state of knowledge in our field. This knowledge is by nature one of dynamic unfolding. Principles suggested in the Guidelines and in the text therefore are to be viewed not as static but as open to continual revision and elaboration. They provide above all a way of thinking about, or an approach to, case management and problem solving. New ideas and practices continue to emerge, brought about by influences as varied as the changing conditions of life, new diseases, changes in legislation, socioeconomic and cultural vicissitudes, and scientific or medical discoveries. It is obvious that no completed or final study of the field of child placement could exist, not only because each instance of child neglect, abuse, or abandonment is as unique and complex as are the individuals involved, but also because child placement conflicts will always mirror the changing conditions of our society. We hope that this book will be of practical use to CPS workers, whose unremitting efforts to help troubled families confront them with human nature in all its difficulty, diversity, and fascination.

Appendix 1

Connecticut's Guidelines for the
Removal and Return of Children*

Standards for the removal and return of children by the Department of Children and Youth Services became effective as Connecticut state policy on January 1, 1981. Informally referred to as the Guidelines (DCYS Bulletin #30; *Manual Volume 2*), the text of the bulletin follows.

Introduction

Although the policy of DCYS is to maintain children in their own homes whenever possible, certain events in the child's life make consideration of either temporary (up to 96 hours) or long-term placement a necessity. Up to this time, the responsibility for such decision-making has rested primarily on the judgment of the individual worker and supervisor. To ensure consistent implementation of the law throughout the State of Connecticut, and to help DCYS workers in making difficult decisions, DCYS and the Yale University Child Study Center have worked cooperatively to develop the following guidelines for use by DCYS workers in considering the removal and return of children for whom placement is indicated.

Many families demonstrate child neglect or other problems that do not ordinarily warrant the removal of a child from the home. The following guidelines apply only to the decision to remove a child from his home, and should *not* be construed as limiting access to services that are available on a voluntary basis. On the contrary,

*These currently are under review to adapt them to newer knowledge and the lessons learned in applying them over the years.

it is expected that the public and private sectors will work together to ensure the provision of the full spectrum of voluntary services needed to provide meaningful support to children and families.* We must emphasize that if services are truly voluntary, the simple refusal to accept services does not constitute cause for removal, or even for further extended inquiry into the family's situation.

The primary assumption of the following guidelines is that every child needs and deserves to feel secure in his or her home environment. Security involves both the physical and emotional well-being of the child. Enduring relationships and continuity of care are essential to a child's healthy development.†

Therefore, removal is a drastic step. The following process should be used to consider other alternatives prior to removing a child:

> For non-emergency cases, the process of decision-making should begin with a conference between the worker, the supervisor, and the program supervisor (or a second supervisor). For emergency placement, such a conference should take place within two working days of the temporary removal of the child. Plans should be developed based on the child's age and developmental needs. Written plans, including the reasons behind them, should be entered in the child's record.
>
> Such conferences should be a time to discuss, for example, danger to the child or child's needs that are not met; support mechanisms for the family (both those which are available in the community and those ideally available); what placement options are available if the decision to remove the

*See page 70ff.
†For background reading on these psychological tenets, see Goldstein et al. 1973 and 1979. Further references are cited in both volumes.

child is made; the number of siblings in the family and the possible impact on them; or what special needs, if any, the child presents.

Each individual case will require a specific assessment of the parent and child. Assessments should involve the least disturbing and most constructive individual consideration of each parent and child. During the course of these evaluations, sensitivity should be shown to the fact that an evaluation in itself can disrupt and undermine family life.

All assessments resulting in the removal of a child must be thoroughly reviewed administratively every three months for children 0–5 years of age and every six months for children 6–18 years of age. This assumes that each such case is being clinically reviewed by the staff worker and her/his supervisor at least once a month. These reviews should again include the worker, supervisor, and program supervisor who should consider any changes in the circumstances of the family or child. Again, a written record should be kept in the case file.

If a decision is made to remove the child, the process described on page 4 of these guidelines must be followed immediately.

Presumptions to Guide Decision-Making

Presumption 1: If a child has been physically or sexually assaulted (so that the child's life or physical safety is threatened), the presumption is that the child must be assured of being in a safer environment. An exception to removing the child may be warranted when the following two conditions are met:

(a) Assessment is adequate to identify the factors that caused the abuse and the parents are able to make changes or use services that will prevent a recurrence (e.g., dismissing an abusive babysitter, leaving an abusive boyfriend).

(b) There are sufficient services to reduce significantly the risk of remaining in the home until either long-term services or a change in those who care for the child can assure that the child's life is now safeguarded.

If the assessment and the service (as described in a and b above) are not adequate, the child must be safeguarded by separating the child and the adult suspected of committing the assault by removing either the suspected adult or the child.

Presumption 2: When DCYS is considering moving a child out of the child's current placement (whether that is a biological or foster home, or an institution) several conditions for long-range planning should be met:

(a) DCYS should be able to identify a specific alternative for the child; and

(b) that specific alternative should be a more appropriate and, above all, a safer placement than the one in which the child currently resides.

Guidelines for Removal of Children

I. Emergency or Immediate Removal (for 96 Hours or Less—Temporary Hold)

Process: Initial Assessment and Decision at Once

Reasons:

1. Non-accidental serious physical injury

2. Sexual assault with physical injury

3. Abandonment, whether voluntary or involuntary

4. Physically demonstrated threat to life, e.g., a physically demonstrated threat of dropping a baby from a window; or of attacking a child with a weapon; or situations in which a realistic appraisal indicates the overwhelming likelihood of immediate physical danger to the child.

Examples of injuries serious enough to indicate a possible threat to life include, but are not limited to:

significant burns

wounds from a stabbing or shooting

severe lacerations

ruptured viscera (damaged internal organs)

broken bones

any series of injuries in which the child has experienced a pattern of "accidents" or unexplained injuries that could have been prevented

For all of the above, medical consultation shall be obtained.

II. Planned Removal (Planned over Several Days, Weeks, or Months)

Process: Inquiry/Assessment/Decision

Several conditions and situations raise the question of whether the child may need to be removed from the home after careful investigation.

For purposes of planned removal, *imminent risk* shall be defined as a situation in which the behavior of the adult caretakers, whether by omission or commission, threatens serious damage to the child or endangers the child's life.

Reasons:

1. Existing serious physical damage or imminent risk of serious physical damage due to severe neglect.

2. Imminent risk of physical or sexual assault likely to entail serious damage to the child.

Case workers should examine *how* the sexual relationship occurred as well as *that it did*. Sexual assault is a particularly important area in which to consider removing the offending adult rather than the child from the home. All suspected cases of sexual assault should be reported to the appropriate authorities.

3. Imminent risk of abandonment.

4. Natural or foster parents want to have children removed.

Children should be removed only if they are not wanted, not

because parents who want their children feel forced to give them up because of economic need or because of a lack of supportive services. Runaway behavior of older children that expresses their urgent wish to be placed outside of the family could be construed to meet this criterion for planned removal if the parents are in agreement.

The Ongoing Process: Once a Decision to Remove Is Made

1. If the decision is made to remove the child and the possibility exists for returning the child to the parents, arrangements must be made *immediately* to maintain *frequent contact* between parent and child.

2. A social service plan of action between *DCYS and the parent* must be developed to explain why the child has been removed, what behavior and circumstances need to be changed for the child to be returned, and this plan of action is a dated, written agreement outlining both short-term and long-term intentions and detailed specific responsibilities for both DCYS and the parent(s). The plan of action should be agreed to mutually and signed by both parties. It is intended to provide guidance for the parents and the DCYS, not to be used as a legally-binding document.*

3. If the child is placed in a foster home, the *foster parent* needs to be involved in working with the child and the parents in preparing for the child's return.

4. *For children* who can return home, plans need to be developed based on the child's age and developmental needs. The worker and supervisor must develop a process for review and monitoring.

5. *Planning* for the return of the child *should include*:
   (a) consideration of the reasons for removal, and

---

*Repeated failures of this service may necessitate changes in case management to ensure expeditious placement decisions on behalf of the child.

(b) an assessment of the child's attachments to all significant parent and sibling figures.

6. When planning for the return of children, the social worker must consider the use of ongoing community support programs and systems, and the phasing-out of the direct involvement of DCYS with the client.

7. For children who cannot be returned home, planning for permanent placement must be instituted immediately.

Planning for Return or Non-Return of Children Placed Outside of Their Own Homes

The first option for all children should be to return home.

1. Planning for return should be placed in a time frame based on the developmental needs of the individual child; e.g., the younger the child the more urgent the need for implementation of a permanent plan.

2. Planning for the return of the child should include:
   (a) an assessment of the child's attachments to all significant parent and sibling figures; and
   (b) a review of the reasons for removal, and evaluation of changes in the family's situation that would assure the child a safe and nurturing environment.

While it is assumed that most children should be returned home, it is presumed that children in the following categories should *not* be returned home. Once this presumption is reached, immediate legal action shall be taken.

1. Those children who have been placed outside of their homes because of life-threatening injuries at the hands of the adults responsible for them should not be returned to those adults. Children in that extreme situation will never feel emotionally secure with the adults who attacked them, even if their physical safety could be assured.

The department should file co-terminous petitions for these children.

2. When children have established primary or very strong relationships with surrogate parents, have lost their primary relationships to their biological parents or never developed such relationships, and when the surrogate parents are prepared to keep them permanently and a clinical judgment is made that the children's long-range development will be threatened by their removal from the surrogate parents, all efforts should be made within the law to enable those children to remain with the surrogate parents.

Appendix 2

Child Welfare Work in Connecticut*

In Connecticut, the Department of Children and Youth Services (DCYS) was established in 1970 to administer the juvenile delinquency programs in the state. In 1974, DCYS was expanded by order of the General Assembly to assume responsibility for protective services and mental health services for children, which previously had been administered by the State Welfare Department.

Protective Services is a specialized service extended to families on behalf of children under 18 years of age who are neglected, abused, or abandoned. It is distinguished from other services provided by DCYS and other community agencies in that it is involuntary; the parents or guardian of the child usually have not asked for help, and the Department cannot leave them free to decide whether they want help or not. The primary goals of Protective Services are to ensure that children are protected from physical harm and that parents can function independently and adequately in providing care for their children.

It is the Department's policy (in compliance with Public Law 96-272, effective October 1, 1980, implemented in Connecticut in 1983) to make every effort to prevent or eliminate the need for removing the child from his home. Once a child is removed, the Department must make every effort to facilitate his return. If return home is not possible, an alternative permanent plan for the child must be quickly developed.

The Department's legal mandate states that it must discharge its authority in a professional, nonthreatening, and nonpunitive fashion. The Department has the legal obligation to act upon all

*Summary of legal requirements concerning child abuse and neglect from General Statutes of Connecticut, revised January 1, 1991, Volume 6, P-194, Section 17a-3.

received reports of suspected child abuse, neglect, and/or abandonment.

The Department has the right to:

1. Intervene in situations which warrant community concern on behalf of the child, although the family is not seeking such intervention;

2. Assess the facts;

3. Offer help although it may not be wanted or accepted;

4. Make clear that the community cannot allow a situation harmful to a child to persist;

5. Remain involved with the child until there is no further need to be concerned about the child's immediate well-being;

6. Take legal action, when necessary, through the Superior Court–Juvenile Matters. This should be done when it is determined that (1) conditions in the home cannot be changed because of parental inability or unwillingness to use the service offered or (2) despite the parents' willingness to accept help, the time needed to effect change would exceed the child's capacity to wait, or (3) the conditions of abuse/neglect are overwhelmingly damaging.

A summary of the legal requirements of the State of Connecticut concerning child abuse/neglect is as follows:

The public policy of the State of Connecticut is to protect children whose health and welfare may be affected adversely through injury and neglect; to strengthen the family and to make the home safe for children by enhancing the parental capacity for good child care; to provide a temporary or permanent nurturing and safe environment for children when necessary; and, for these purposes, to require the reporting of suspected child abuse, investigation of such reports by a social agency, and provision of services, where needed, to such child and family [17-38a].*

*Specific citations from the Connecticut general statutes are noted in brackets.

Who Is *Mandated* to Report Child Abuse-Neglect?

Chiropractors, Clergymen, Coroners, Day Care Employees, Dentists, Hospital Interns, Hospital Residents, Licensed Practical Nurses, Medical Examiners, Mental Health Professionals, Optometrists, Osteopaths, Physicians, Podiatrists, Police Officers, Psychologists, Registered Nurses, School Guidance Counselors, School Principals, School Teachers, Social Workers, Surgeons [17-38a (b)]

Do Those Mandated to Report Incur Liability?

No. Any person, institution, or agency reporting in good faith is immune from any liability, civil or criminal [17-38a (h)].

Is There a Penalty for Not Reporting?

Yes. A person required to report who fails to do so shall be fined not more than $500 [17-38a (b)].

What Is the Reporting Procedure?

1. An oral report must be made *immediately* to the Commissioner of DCYS or his representatives or to the local or state police [17-38a (c)].

2. A *written* report must follow within *72 hours*. It can be submitted to a DCYS regional office or directly to the Commissioner at the central office [17-38a (c)].

3. If a person is making the report as a member of the staff of a hospital, school, social agency or other institution, the reporter *also* must notify the head of the institution or his designee that such a report has been made [17-38a (b)].

4. All information, if known by the reporter, must be reported [17-38a (c)].

5. Agencies or institutions receiving reports must transfer such information to the Commissioner of DCYS or his agent *within 24 hours* [17-38a (e)].

What Must Be Reported?

1. *Child Abuse*: defined as any child under the age of 18 who has had physical injury or injuries inflicted upon him by a person responsible for his health, welfare or care or by a person given access to the child by the responsible person other than by accidental means or has injuries which are at variance with the history given of them, or is in a condition which is the result of maltreatment such as, but not limited to, malnutrition, sexual molestation, deprivation of necessities, emotional maltreatment or cruel punishment or who has been neglected [17-38a (b) and 17-53].

2. *Child Neglect*: defined as any child under 18 who has been abandoned or is being denied proper care and attention, physically, emotionally or morally, or is being permitted to live under conditions, circumstances or associations injurious to his well-being or who has been abused [17-53].

Exception: The treatment of any child by an accredited Christian Science practitioner shall not, of itself, constitute neglect or maltreatment [17-53].

3. *Child at Risk*: a child believed to be in danger of being abused, as opposed to a child who has actually been abused [17-38 (b)].

4. *Child under 13 with VD*: a physician or facility must report to the Commissioner of DCYS on the consultation, examination, and treatment for venereal disease of any child not more than 12 years old [19-89a].

Do Private Citizens Have a Responsibility for Reporting?

Yes. A separate section of the law indicates that any person, in addition to those specifically mandated, shall give an oral or written report to DCYS when there is reasonable cause to suspect child abuse/neglect. Such a person making the report in good faith also is immune from any liability, civil or criminal. There is, however, no penalty for not reporting [17-38c].

What Are the Authority and Responsibility of the
Department of Children and Youth Services?

1. All children's protective services are the responsibility of
DCYS.

2. Upon the receipt of a child abuse-neglect report, DCYS
shall investigate immediately.

3. If the investigation produces evidence of child abuse/ne-
glect, DCYS shall take such measures as it deems necessary to
protect the child and *any other children similarly situated*, including,
but not limited to, the removal of the child or children *with* the
consent of the parents or guardian or by order of the Juvenile
Court.

4. If DCYS has probable cause to believe the child is suffering
from serious physical illness or serious physical injury or is in immediate physical danger from his surroundings and that immediate removal is necessary to ensure the child's safety, *the
Commissioner of DCYS or his designee may authorize any department
employee or any law enforcement officer to remove the child without the
consent of the parent or guardian.* Such removal and temporary custody cannot exceed *96 hours*, during which time the Commissioner
either must file a petition with the Juvenile Court or return the
child to his parents.

5. If the child is returned to the parents, they shall be aided to
give proper care under the supervision of the Commissioner until
the Commissioner finds that a safe environment has been provided
[17-38a (e)].

What Means Are Available for Removing a Child from His Home?

1. *96 hour* hold by the Commissioner of DCYS (see #4 above).

2. *96 hour custody by a hospital.* Any physician examining a child
with respect to suspected abuse may retain the child for 96 hours
under the custody of a hospital with or *without* the consent of the
parents or guardian pending study of the family and home by the
welfare agency concerned or the filing of a petition to the Juvenile

Court. The costs of the hospital stay will be paid by DCYS if the parents or guardian are unable to do so [17-38a (d)].

3. *Superior Court Seven-Day Custody Order.* Whenever a person is arrested and charged with any of the following offenses [against an adult or a child] 1) cruelty to persons [53-20], 2) risk of injury [53-21], 3) assault and related offenses [Chapter 952, Part V], 4) sex offenses [Chapter 952, Part VI], or 5) kidnapping or related offenses [Chapter 952, Part VII] and if the victim was a minor residing with the defendant, the Superior Court may issue an order to the Commissioner of DCYS to assume immediate custody of such child and, if the circumstances so require, any other children residing with the defendant, for a period of *seven days* giving DCYS the necessary time to petition the Juvenile Court for custody [17-38e].

4. *Juvenile Court* may place in some suitable agency or person the child's temporary care and custody *pending* a hearing of a petition for removal. The hearing must be held within ten days of the order for temporary care and custody [17-62 subsec. b].* In Juvenile Court proceedings, evidence that the child has been abused or has sustained injury shall constitute prima facie evidence that shall be sufficient to support adjudication that the child is uncared for or neglected [17-38a (f)].

What Is the Child Abuse Central Registry?

DCYS is required to maintain a registry and permit its use on a 24-hour daily basis to prevent or discover abuse of children. Required confidentiality is ensured. The registry may be reached by calling CARE-LINE: 1-800-842-2288 [17-38a (q)].

---

*Usually referred to as an OTC (Order of Temporary Custody).

References

Abramovitz, R. Adoption enlightenment. Unpublished manuscript.

————. Communicating with children of alternative conception. Unpublished manuscript.

Adams-Tucker, C. 1984. The unmet psychiatric needs of sexually abused youths: Referrals from a child protection agency and clinical evaluations. *J. Amer. Acad. Child Psychiat.* 23:659–667.

Andersen, R. S. 1988. Why adoptees search: Motives and more. *Child Welfare* 67:15–19.

Caffey, J. 1946. Multiple fractures in the long bones of infants suffering from chronic subdural hematoma. *Amer. J. Roentgenology* 56:163–173.

————. 1957. Some traumatic lesions in growing bones other than fractures and dislocations: Clinical and radiological features. *Brit. J. Radiology* 30:225–238.

Caplan, L. 1990. *An Open Adoption.* New York: Farrar, Straus, and Giroux.

Cohen, S. J., and Sussman, A. 1975. The incidence of child abuse in the United States. Report submitted to the Office of Child Development, Washington, D.C.

Coleman, S. H. 1924. *Humane Society Leaders in America.* Albany, N.Y.: American Humane Association.

Crewdson, J. 1988. *By Silence Betrayed.* Boston: Little, Brown.

Gerbner, G., Ross, C. J., and Zigler, E. 1980. *Child Abuse: An Agenda for Action.* New York: Oxford University Press.

Goldstein, J., Freud, A., and Solnit, A. J. 1973. *Beyond the Best Interests of the Child.* New York: Free Press.

————. 1979. *Before the Best Interests of the Child.* New York: Free Press.

Hiner, N. R. 1979. Children's rights, corporal punishment, and child abuse. *Bull. Menninger Clin.* 43:233–248.

Kaufman, J., and Zigler, E. F. 1987. Do abused children become abusive parents? *Amer. J. Orthopsychiat.* 57:186–192.

Lewis, M. B., and Sorrel, P. M. 1968. The management of sexual assault upon children. In *Ambulatory Pediatrics,* ed. M. Green and R. J. Haggerty. Philadelphia: W. B. Saunders.

Mnookin, R. H. 1978. *Child, Family and State*. Boston: Little, Brown.

Nagi, S. 1975. Child abuse neglect programs: A national overview. *Children Today* 4:13–18.

Radbill, S. X. 1980. A history of child abuse and infanticide. In *The Battered Child*, ed. R. E. Helfer and C. H. Kempe. Chicago: University of Chicago Press.

Secretary of State for Social Services. 1988. Report of the Inquiry into Child Abuse in Cleveland 1987. London: Her Majesty's Stationery Office.

Solnit, A. J. 1980. Too much reporting, too little service: Roots and prevention of child abuse. Pp. 135–146 in *Child Abuse: An Agenda for Action*, ed. G. Gerbner, C. J. Ross, and E. Zigler. New York: Oxford University Press.

Sorosky, A. D., Baron, A., and Pannor, R. 1978. *The Adoption Triangle*. Garden City, N.Y.: Anchor Press/Doubleday.

Ward, M. 1984. Sibling ties in foster care and adoption planning. *Child Welfare* 63:321–332.

Index

Abandonment, 17, 24, 43–44, 85–87, 110, 124–25, 135, 139, 141, 170

Abduction of children by parents, 91

Abramovitz, R., 109

Abuse: case of Mary Ellen, 3–4; cases pertaining to life-threatening injuries, 29–42; children's memory of, 103–04; cycle of, 4–5, 59; definition of, 170; denial by parents, 34, 37, 39, 105–06; denial by professionals, 39–41; denial by public, 4; false reports of, 7, 74–75; fatal outcome of, 75–78; of handicapped children, 39–42, 56–58, 62–65; historical perspectives on, 3–4; of infants, 33–39, 42–44, 49–56, 59–61, 106–09; laws concerning, 5–7, 168–72; mistaken identification of, 66–70; national center on, 7; psychological roots of, 4–5; reporting of, 4, 14; statistics on, 7. *See also* Neglect; Parents; Sexual abuse

Adams-Tucker, C., 83

Adolescence/Adolescents: girls' needs for mother, 95, 96–98; needs of, 12, 15, 141, 152, 153; sexual abuse of, 94–99

Adoption, 22, 150, 152; adoptee's curiosity about birth parents, 111–13, 149–53; of biracial children, 119–27; birth parents' role in, 110–11; cases pertaining to, 35–36, 38–39, 48, 52, 59–61, 114–27, 149–53; exit process and dynamics, 149–53; informing child of, 109, 113–14, 149; laws concerning, 110, 112; myths concerning, 110; open adoption, 112; as placement alternative, 22; principles of, 109–14; and sealed birth records, 110, 112; of siblings, 114–19; subsidized adoption, 56; threat of disrupted adoption, 114–19

Adulthood, 12. *See also* Fathers; Mothers; Parents; Relatives; Workers

AIDS, 82, 144–47

Alcohol abuse, cases involving, 39–44, 59–61, 73, 85, 144

Ambivalence: of parent-foster parent, 40, 77, 130; of professional, 117

American Society for the Prevention of Cruelty to Animals, 3

"Anatomically correct" dolls, 84

Andersen, R., 113

Anger: of children, 48, 76, 81,